ORIENTAL
COOKBOOK

By the same author

Spicy and Delicious

Priya Wickramasinghe

ORIENTAL COOKBOOK

J.M. Dent & Sons Ltd
London Melbourne Toronto

First published 1982
© 1982 Priya Wickramasinghe

Phototypeset in 11 on 13pt Monophoto Photina by
Servis Filmsetting Ltd, Manchester
Printed in Great Britain by
Richard Clay (The Chaucer Press) Ltd, Bungay, for
J.M. Dent & Sons Ltd
Aldine House 33 Welbeck Street London W1M 8LX

British Library Cataloguing in Publication Data

Wickramasinghe, Priya
  Oriental cookbook.
  1. Cookery, Oriental
  I. Title
  641.595   TX724.5.A1

  ISBN 0–460–04510–5

Contents

Introduction

The Orient includes much of Asia, the world's largest continent, extending from the eastern foothills of the Ural mountains all the way to the Pacific Ocean and south to the Indian Ocean. It occupies nearly one-third of the earth's total land area, and its people account for well over two-thirds of the world's population. Asia also includes many offshore islands such as Sri Lanka, the Maldives, Indonesia, the Philippines, Taiwan and Japan.

Scattered throughout this vast continent are peoples of many distinct races and religions, occupying a wide range of geographical terrains – coastal plains, deserts, mountains – with varying climatic conditions. The Orient also has a rich diversity of cultures, social customs and, of course, culinary styles. Over the centuries there has been a steady migration of peoples from one Oriental country to another – and such popular movement still continues. Consequently, there has been an inevitable degree of mixing of culinary styles, and a tendency to evolve, adapt and merge. Despite such intermingling, distinctive national characteristics have remained discernible, contributing to gastronomic variety and the spice of life.

Chinese cooking is significantly different from Indian cooking, and Indian cooking in turn differs fundamentally from the culinary styles of Indonesia and Malaysia. Similarities of cuisine exist, particularly between countries that are geographically adjacent or climatically similar, or between cultures that are closely related. Thus Indian and Sri Lankan cooking share a common cultural heritage, although they are by no means identical. There are common features between Sri Lankan and Indonesian food; and Chinese and Japanese food have obvious areas of overlap.

The availability of common spices and basic raw materials often makes for close similarities of food and culinary styles. Rice, which is the major cereal crop, forms the staple diet across much of Asia. Noodles, made of wheat flour, compete for pride of place with rice, particularly in certain parts of China and South East Asia. Wherever the coconut is grown it is used abundantly in cooking, for instance in Sri Lanka and Indonesia. Soya beans, along with the many products derived from them, serve to link the eating habits of China, Taiwan, Japan and other countries of the Far East. And these are only a few examples of the interrelationships between Oriental culinary styles. All in all, Asia boasts a rich variety of foods and methods of preparation, giving the adventurous cook tremendous scope for gastronomical exploration.

Modern air travel has brought the whole of Asia literally to our doorstep, no matter where we may live. The twentieth-century world has shrunk astonishingly: access to once-distant and remote places is now limited only by the size of our purses and, perhaps, our capacity for adventure. Large numbers of tourists and businessmen travel daily back and forth between the capital cities of West and East: such far-flung cities as Bombay, Colombo, Singapore, Hong Kong and Tokyo are only hours away from London or Paris.

Along with easy access has come a new awareness of Oriental culture and a surge of Western interest in Oriental food and Oriental cooking. Chinese, Indian and Indonesian restaurants abound, and eating out Oriental-style is commonplace. But for the adventurous and imaginative cook the preparation of Oriental dishes at home is just as easy, and a good deal more rewarding. All the ingredients which are needed for such cooking are readily available at Chinese and Indian grocery stores, or in any specialist food store or delicatessen. These include a vast and impressive array of exotic spices, Indian and Chinese fruits and vegetables, lentils, rice and noodles.

The equipment used in the average Western kitchen more than suffices to replace traditional utensils – often more primitive – used by an Asian cook. For Chinese-style cooking you may like to invest in a wok, and for Indian cooking an iron griddle for frying and an electric coffee grinder to be set aside for grinding spices, may come in handy.

I have grouped recipes under functional headings – Soups, Poultry dishes, Sweets, etc. – rather than separate them according to countries. In this way it would be possible to construct for yourself hybrid menu combinations, including items from different countries. (See the chapter at the end of the book on Suggested Menu Combinations.) I have, however, indicated the country where each recipe comes from, and also in most cases given a brief comment about the dish itself. Each recipe has been carefully tested, and found to be practicable for preparation in a Western kitchen. The selection of recipes in a book such as this must necessarily be a somewhat personal matter. Criteria for my own selection have been dictated by the range of my travels in the Orient, what I have eaten and liked in these various countries, together with an assessment of what I consider relevant in a Western context.

Ingredients

The ingredients used in Oriental cooking vary widely from one country to another. Basic raw materials such as rice, pulses and beans are common to many countries, but the seasonings and spices used are dependent on local availability and are quite variable. The varieties of vegetable, poultry, meat, fish and shellfish that are used also differ from one part to another. Most types of vegetable, meat and fish that are available in the West lend themselves to preparation in exotic styles that characterize the different parts of Asia. Indian and Chinese vegetables and other commodities are also fairly easily obtainable in the West, for specialist grocery stores that stock such goods can now be found in large numbers in all our major cities.

Items such as onions, garlic and ginger, which are extensively used in Oriental cooking, are so familiar to us in the West that they need no comment, but the liberal use of many of these ingredients in Oriental cooking might come as something of a surprise. Together with a range of spices they make for the varied and distinctive flavours that characterize Oriental cooking. Many of the spices used – cinnamon, cardamom, cloves, chilli – are already quite familiar to the Western cook. But there are others that are less familiar, although nonetheless readily available. I list below, in alphabetical order, those spices and other ingredients that I consider somewhat atypical of Western cooking.

Aburagé Japanese fried bean curd, which is available in the form of thin sheets.

Agar Agar A gelatine extracted from seaweed. Used as a setting agent in Chinese, Japanese and Burmese desserts, it is readily available at Chinese grocery stores.

Ajinomoto See *Monosodium Glutamate*.

Aka-Miso A red bean paste used in Japanese cooking.

Allspice Partly dried berries of *Pimenta dioica*, a tropical tree of the myrtle family. Allspice is used more in Western cooking than in Eastern cuisine. It owes its name to the belief that it combines the flavours of cinnamon, cloves and nutmeg.

Aniseed This spice is widely grown throughout Asia and is used in curries in a roasted form (cumin seed).

Asafoetida This pungently smelling resin is obtained from the root of the herb *Ferula foetida*. It is cultivated widely in the Middle East and it is used in many vegetable dishes.

Bamboo Shoots The shoots of young bamboos are collected before they emerge from the ground. If fresh bamboo shoots are used they must be boiled for a long time until cooked; they are available already cooked in most Chinese grocery stores.

Bean Curd See *Soya Bean Curd*.

Bean Sprouts The white young sprouts from germinating soya beans or other types of bean such as mung beans. You could sprout these yourself or buy ready sprouted beans from Chinese grocery stores and supermarkets.

Blachan A paste made from dried and salted shrimps or prawns. This is a basic flavouring used throughout most of South East Asia.

Bonito Flakes (Katsuobushi) Dried fish flakes used in Japanese cooking.

Capsicum or sweet pepper, is used for curries, but it is not hot or pungent like chilli.

Caraway These are black seeds which have a distinctive flavour, slightly resembling aniseed. It is not too frequently used in curries.

Cardamom These are seeds of a herb of the ginger family. Whole cardamom pods are used for flavouring rice, but these should be removed before serving. For curries the seeds are removed from the pods and ground. In some parts of India, cardamom is used for flavouring tea and coffee. It is also chewed after meals as a breath-sweetener.

Cayenne Pepper This is made by grinding the dried pods and seeds of *Capsicum frutescens* and *Capsicum minimum* to a fine powder. It is darker than paprika and very much hotter. Cayenne pepper is a good substitute for chilli.

Chilli This is a small, very hot variety of capsicum (*Capsicum annum*) which can be either red or green. Dried red pods are used whole or ground to make chilli powder. Either whole chillies or chilli powder can be used in curries. This single ingredient is responsible for the hotness of curries.

Chinese Cabbage Several types are used in Chinese cooking, most of them available in Chinese grocery stores.

Chinese Mushrooms These have a characteristically strong flavour, and are readily available in Chinese grocery stores.

Chinese Vermicelli A fine, clear type of noodle made from gram or pea flour. Readily available.

Cinnamon This fragrant spice is the dried bark of *Cinnamomum zeylanicum*, grown mainly in Sri Lanka. It is an important ingredient of curries, and it is also used in sweet dishes.

Cloves These dried unopened flower buds of *Eugenia caryophyllata* or *Myrtus caryophyllata* are a major ingredient in Indian and Sri Lankan cooking. Cloves were an important commodity in the spice trade.

Coriander This is derived from the plant *Coriandrum sativum*. Its leaves are used for garnishing dishes and the crushed seeds are used in curry powder.

Creamed Coconut Solidified extract of the coconut kernel. It is readily available in Indian and Chinese food stores. Coconut milk, which is frequently used in South East Asian cookery, can be made instantly by dissolving creamed coconut in hot water.

Cumin The seeds of black cumin (*Cuminum nigrum*) and white cumin (*Cuminum cyminum*) are ground and used in many sweet and savoury dishes.

Curry Leaves The leaves of *Murraya koenigii*, a small shrub of the orange family, are often used in curries, particularly in South India and Sri Lanka. They add a characteristic fragrance and flavour.

Daikon A large white radish which is used extensively in Japanese cookery. It is available in specialist foodstores in the West.

Dashi, Dashinomoto A clear stock made from seaweed and dried bonito flakes. Available at Japanese and Chinese grocery stores.

Fennel This herb is thought to be one of the oldest used by man. Ground seeds of *Foeniculum vulgare* are used in curries. Fresh or dried seeds are also chewed after a meal as a digestive or breath-sweetener.

Fenugreek This spice is derived from the plant *Trigonella foenum-graecum*, a member of the pea family. Roasted, ground fenugreek seeds are used in curry powder.

Garam Masala This is the name given to a mixture of spices used for curries. Commercially mixed garam masala is obtainable from Indian grocery stores. Recipes for making your own garam masala from individual spices are given under *Basic Recipes*.

Ghee Clarified butter – readily available in Indian grocery stores. See instructions under *Basic Recipes* for making your own ghee.

Ginger This is the root of the herbaceous plant *Zingiber officinalis* which is used extensively in Indian and Sri Lankan cooking. Fresh ginger (called 'green' ginger) is to be preferred to dried ginger powder.

Glutinous Rice/Flour A variety of rice/rice flour which becomes sticky when cooked. Available in Chinese shops.

Gula Melaka See *Jaggery*.

Hoi Sin Sauce A sweet spicy sauce with a russet colour, made from soya beans, garlic and spices.

Jaggery This sweetening agent, obtained from various types of palm, is used for making many Sri Lankan and other South East Asian desserts.

Kamaboku Japanese fish sausage, available in cans.

Kapi Also called blachan by Malays and trasi by Indonesians, this is a paste made from prawns. It is available in specialist stores.

Kombu A type of Japanese dried seaweed.

Konnyaku Starchy extract from the roots of a vegetable. It comes in two forms – canned in the form of soft cubes and as fine noodles called shirataki. The noodle form is a must for the famous Japanese dish 'Sukiyaki'.

Laos Powder A powder made from *Alpinia galanga*, a root similar to ginger.

Lemon Grass This highly fragrant tropical grass can be made to grow in pots indoors. Not always easily available, but grated lemon rind may be used instead.

Lentil There are many types of lentil used in Indian cooking, including chana dhal, moong dhal and urad dhal. They are readily available in Indian grocery stores.

Lily Buds Available in dried form in Chinese grocery stores.

Macadamia Nuts These nuts are used raw in Malaysian and Indonesian cooking. When they are not available, blanched almonds may be substituted quite successfully.

Mace The lacy outer covering of the nutmeg (see below).

Maldive Fish Dried fish from the Maldive Islands is used in many Sri Lankan curries. It is sold in Indian grocery stores.

Mirin A sweet Japanese rice wine used in cooking, available in Far Eastern food stores. A sweet sherry would probably be an acceptable alternative, at a pinch.

Miso Cooked and fermented soya beans made into a paste. Japanese soups are thickened with it. Often sold in health food shops.

Monosodium Glutamate (MSG) This chemical is used extensively in Far Eastern cooking, to bring out flavours. It should be used sparingly.

Mustard Seed The small dark brown seed of *Brassica juncea* is used whole and fried in hot oil in the preparation of most curries. Mustard oil is also used in cooking, particularly in Bengal.

Nam Prik, Nam Pla Fish sauces used in Thai cooking, readily available in Chinese supermarkets.

Noodles A rice substitute, extensively used in Chinese cooking. Usually made of wheat flour.

Nori A variety of Japanese seaweed.

Nutmeg The seed of the evergreen tree, known as *Myristica fragrans*, grown in Sri Lanka and throughout the Malay archipelago. Grated nutmeg is used both in curries and sweet dishes.

Pandams Leaf This leaf is used extensively in South East Asian cooking, to flavour rice and curries, and particularly for sweets in Malaysia and Indonesia.

Pepper This most familiar spice comes from a vine which is native to Sri Lanka, South India and Malaya. Dried berries become peppercorns, which can be ground.

Poppy Seeds Seeds of the opium poppy (*Papaver somniferum*) are often added to curry powders. They have no smell, but a nutty flavour. They are believed to stimulate the appetite!

Prawns, Dried Available in most Chinese shops.

Rose Essence Extract of rose petals. It is used to flavour sweet dishes in India and Pakistan. Available from chemist's shops and from Eastern food stores.

Saffron The dried stamen of *Crocus sativus* is one of the most expensive of spices. Saffron gives a dish a delicate aroma and a golden yellow colour. A very minute quantity (one or two stamens) goes a long way.

Sake Japanese rice wine. Available at specialist foodstores and wine merchants.

Serai Powder Dried lemon grass in a powdered form. See *Lemon Grass*.

Sesame Seeds Seeds from the herbaceous plant *Sesamum indicum*, extensively used in Indian cooking. Oil from this seed is called gingerly oil and is used for frying. The powdered seeds are often mixed into curry powders.

Sesame Oil Used as a flavouring agent – not as cooking oil.

Shirataki Very fine cellophane noodles.

Soya Bean Curd A soft white cheese used extensively in Chinese and Japanese cooking. Available in Chinese grocery stores.

Soy Sauce A basic flavouring used throughout the Far East, available in bottles.

Tamarind The dried fruit of the Tamarind tree (*Tamarindus indica*) can be soaked in hot water to extract its tart acidic juice. This extract is then used for cooking curry dishes.

Tofu Bean curd, made from soya beans. Tofu normally comes in

the form of jelly-like flavourless blocks, sold in Chinese
supermarkets. It can be stored, immersed in cold water, in a
refrigerator for about three days. An instant Japanese variety comes
in the form of a powder and has to be reconstituted by mixing with
water. A good protein substitute.

Trasi See *Kapi*.

Turmeric The root of *Circuma longa*, a member of the ginger family,
is dried and ground into a brilliant yellow coloured powder. It is
used as a flavouring and colouring in curries.

Wasabi Powder Powdered dried horseradish, used in Japanese
cooking.

Water Chestnut A Chinese vegetable with a crisp texture. Canned
water chestnut is readily available.

Basic Recipes

There are certain recipes that are used so often that they warrant grouping under the heading of *Basic Recipes*. These recipes are given in the pages that follow.

Boiled Rice

This is the best way of making fluffy white rice to be served with curries

1 cup rice (washed in a sieve under running cold water until the water runs clear)
2 cups water
1 teaspoonful salt

Put the rice, water and salt in a saucepan and bring to the boil. Stir, cover and simmer for 15 minutes. It is vital that the lid should be kept on for the full 15 minutes.

Serves 4

Garam Masala

For many Indian curries a basic curry powder mix known as garam masala is augmented with individual spices used in varying proportions. Ready mixed garam masala is available in most Indian grocery stores and is perfectly acceptable as a basic mix. However, you might prefer to make your own and there are several tested recipes to choose from. I list here four recipes that I have found quite satisfactory.

Recipe 1

2 tablespoonsful coriander seeds
2 tablespoonsful cumin seeds
1 teaspoonful each fenugreek, mustard seeds and poppy seeds
2 teaspoonsful each cardamom seeds, cloves and dried red chilli
1 tablespoonful black peppercorns
1 tablespoonful turmeric powder
1 tablespoonful ground ginger

Grind all the seeds in a coffee grinder. Add the turmeric and then mix with the ground ginger. Store in an airtight jar.

Recipe 2

4 tablespoonsful coriander seeds
1 tablespoonful cumin seeds
½ tablespoonful cinnamon sticks
1 teaspoonful cardamom seeds
1 teaspoonful cloves
1 teaspoonful nutmeg
1 teaspoonful black peppercorns
½ teaspoonful mace

Roast all the ingredients in a heavy bottomed pan for about 10 minutes. Allow to cool, then grind in a coffee grinder. Store in an airtight jar.

Recipe 3

3 tablespoonsful coriander seeds
3 tablespoonsful cumin seeds
3 tablespoonsful black peppercorns
1 tablespoonful cardamoms
2 teaspoonsful ground cloves
1 tablespoonful ground cinnamon
2 teaspoonsful ground mace

Grind all the ingredients in a coffee grinder. Store in an airtight container.

Recipe 4

4 tablespoonsful ground coriander
2 tablespoonsful ground cumin
1 tablespoonful ground fennel
1 teaspoonful turmeric powder
1 teaspoonful cinnamon powder
1 teaspoonful ground cloves

1 teaspoonful ground cardamom
½ teaspoonful ground fenugreek
1 teaspoonful ground black pepper

Mix thoroughly. Store in an airtight container.

Basic Chinese Stock

I give below a recipe for a basic Chinese chicken stock. By substituting beef bones, or pork bones, or even fish heads and tails for the chicken bones and giblets, you can make beef stock, pork stock or fish stock.

2 pints (1.2 l) cold water
10 black peppercorns
3 slices fresh ginger
1 onion
a few celery stalks
salt to taste
2 lb (900 g) chicken bones, giblets and carcass

Put all the ingredients in a large pan and bring to the boil. Lower the heat to simmer and cook for an hour. Strain the liquid and allow to get cold. Remove all the fat and save only the clear stock.

Yields 2–3 cups

Japanese Chicken Stock

1 small chicken
some chicken bones
1½ teaspoonsful salt
3 spring onions
½ teaspoonful MSG
a small piece of fresh ginger, peeled and sliced
3 pints (1.7 l) water

Put all the ingredients into a large pan and bring to the boil. Reduce the heat and simmer for 1½ hours. Remove the scum from time to time during the cooking. Allow to get cold. Remove any fat and strain through a fine cloth. The stock should be clear and free of any fat.

Yields 1 pint (568 ml)

Dashi (Japanese Fish Soup Stock)

This stock made of dried fish, seaweed and water, forms a basis for most Japanese soups and casseroles. It can be made very easily provided the ingredients are available. An instant version which is available in sachets is certainly a labour-saving substitute. If the idea of a fish stock does not appeal to you, use the same quantity of chicken stock instead in recipes that require dashi.

1 oz (28 g) seaweed (kombu)
10 cups water
1 oz (28 g) dried bonito flakes (katsuobushi)

Wash the seaweed in cold water. In a large pan bring the water to the boil. Add the seaweed and stir it a few times to impregnate the water with its flavour. Bring to the boil and then remove the seaweed. Add the bonito flakes to the water and bring to the boil again. Remove from heat and allow the bonito flakes to settle to the bottom of the pan. Strain and use as required.

Yields approximately 10 cups

Sans Katjang (Peanut Sauce)

This Indonesian peanut sauce is used on sate dishes (meat, grilled on skewers) and on vegetables. Ideally fresh peanuts should be ground to add to the sauce, but the crunchy peanut butter sold in jars is a good substitute.

3 tablespoonsful peanut oil
1 small onion, finely chopped
2 cloves garlic, chopped
3 large dried red chillies, finely chopped
2 teaspoonsful brown sugar
½ teaspoonful salt
2 tablespoonsful soy sauce
1 tablespoonful lemon juice
1 teaspoonful dried shrimp paste
1 lb (454 g) crunchy peanut butter
4 oz (113 g) creamed coconut

Heat the oil and fry the onion in it. Add the garlic and the chillies and fry for a couple of minutes. Add the sugar, salt, soy sauce, lemon juice and shrimp paste and mix thoroughly. Add the peanut butter and lastly the creamed coconut which has been dissolved in two cups of hot water. Simmer the sauce, stirring constantly, until it has become well mixed and thickened.

Yields about 2 cups

Kaeng Kiew Wan (Beef in Green Curry Paste)

A Thai speciality, this green curry paste is sufficient for making a curry with $1\frac{1}{2}$ lb (680 g) of beef. The green chillies make the curry quite hot and should be omitted for those who do not like hot curries.

1 teaspoonful coriander seeds
1 teaspoonful caraway seeds
4 peppercorns
5 green chillies
1 tablespoon lemon grass or lemon rind
1 tablespoonful coriander roots
1 tablespoonful onions, chopped
6 cloves garlic, chopped
$\frac{1}{2}$ teaspoonful salt
$\frac{1}{2}$ teaspoonful kapi
$\frac{1}{2}$ teaspoonful ground turmeric

In a heavy bottomed small frying pan over a low heat roast the coriander seeds, caraway seeds and peppercorns for about 5 minutes or until the seeds become dark brown. Using a pestle and mortar or a small grinder, grind all the ingredients to a smooth paste.

For the curry you will need:

3 oz (85 g) creamed coconut
$1\frac{1}{2}$ cups water
$1\frac{1}{2}$ lb (680 g) stewing beef cut into 1 in (2.5 cm) cubes
2 cardamom pods
1 blade mace
1 bay leaf

In a pan over a medium heat dissolve the creamed coconut in the water. Add the beef, the cardamoms, the mace and bay leaf, and bring to the boil. Simmer, covered, until the meat is tender. Remove the pieces of meat from the pan and bring the liquid to the boil. Add the curry paste and continue to cook the curry sauce until it has thickened and the oil separates and floats on the top. Add the pieces of meat and heat through. Serve with plain boiled rice.

Serves 4

Wonton Wrappers

Wonton wrappers can be bought frozen from Chinese shops. The pastry for these wontons is cut into 3 in (7.5 cm) circles, but this recipe can be used to make spring roll wrappers by cutting the pastry into 6 in (15 cm) squares. Sometimes wontons are made to look like mini cornish pasties.

1 egg
2 fl oz (56 ml) cold water
8 oz (226 g) plain flour
½ teaspoonful salt

Lightly beat the egg. Mix in the cold water. Sieve the flour into a bowl. Add the salt to the flour. Make a well in the centre of the flour and work in the egg and water mixture until you have a ball of soft dough. Knead the dough on a lightly floured surface until smooth. Divide the dough into two. Leave one half covered with a damp cloth. Roll the dough out until the thickness of a postcard. Cut into 3 in (7.5 cm) squares. Store between pieces of greaseproof paper.

Makes 24

Nam Prik

Perhaps the most common of Thai dishes, this can only be described as a hot pungent dipping sauce. A variety of raw or cooked vegetables and steamed or fried fish is served with nam prik and boiled rice. There are many recipes for nam prik with variations in the quantities of chilli, garlic and dried fish. It is very strongly flavoured and may not appeal to everyone.

1 tablespoonful dried shrimps
2 teaspoonsful dried shrimp paste
4 cloves garlic

3 dried red chillies
3 teaspoonsful soft brown sugar
1½ tablespoonsful lime or lemon juice
1 tablespoonful fish sauce (nam pla)

Wash the dried shrimps thoroughly. Wrap the shrimp paste in tin foil and bake at Gas Mark 4/350°F for 4 minutes. Using either a pestle and mortar or an electric blender, mince the shrimps, garlic, chillies and the shrimp paste. Add the sugar, the lime or lemon juice and fish sauce. Serve with a selection of raw or cooked vegetables and steamed or fried fish and plain boiled rice.

Ghee (Clarified Butter)

8 oz (226 g) unsalted butter

Heat the butter in a heavy bottomed pan on a very low heat for about 30 minutes. Remove the floating scum. Strain through muslin into a bowl and allow to cool. Keep in a refrigerator. Use instead of butter or oil.

1

Soups

Chicken Soup

This delicious Japanese soup is a nice warm starter to an Oriental meal.

4 dried mushrooms
2 spring onions
4 oz (113 g) chicken
2 tablespoonsful sake
2 oz (56 g) fine noodles, preferably sōmen
4 cups Japanese chicken stock (see BASIC RECIPES*)*
2 teaspoonsful soy sauce
½ teaspoonful salt

Soak the mushrooms in hot water for 15 minutes and slice them. Wash the spring onions and chop very finely. Cut the chicken into small chunks and marinade in the sake. Cook the noodles according to the instructions on the packet and allow to drain in a colander.

In a saucepan bring the stock to the boil. Add the chicken, mushrooms, soy sauce and salt, and allow to simmer for about 5 minutes or until the chicken is cooked. Finally add the noodles and bring rapidly to the boil. Ladle the soup into four bowls. Garnish with the spring onions.

Serves 4

Chicken Congee

Congee is a rice gruel eaten extensively in China. It is easily digestible and is sometimes given to invalids. In its humblest form it is only a handful of rice boiled for a long time in lots of water, but the recipe given below is a nourishing and wholesome soup.

2 oz (56 g) long grain rice
basic chicken stock (see BASIC RECIPES*)*
1 teaspoonful salt
4 oz (113 g) cooked chicken meat
2 spring onions, finely sliced

Wash the rice in a sieve until the water that runs is clear. Bring the stock and two cups of water to the boil. Add the rice and the salt and simmer, partially covered, for 1 hour. Cut the chicken into bite-sized pieces and add to the rice. Continue to cook for a further 15 minutes. Just prior to serving garnish with spring onions.

Serves 4

Thai Chicken and Rice Soup

A starter and main course combined!

2 lb (1 kg) uncooked chicken backs (carcass excluding legs and breasts) and
    giblets
8 cups water
1 teaspoonful salt
¾ cup rice
2 cups water
1½ tablespoonsful fish sauce (nam pla)
¼ teaspoonful ground black pepper
6 eggs
2 spring onions, finely chopped
1 sprig coriander leaves, for garnishing

Put the chicken, the eight cups of water and salt into a large saucepan and bring to the boil. Cover and simmer for about 2 hours. Strain the chicken stock. Remove any chicken meat from the bones and reserve it. Put the rice and two cups of cold water into a pan and bring rapidly to the boil. Cover and simmer for 30 minutes or until all the water has evaporated. Bring the chicken stock to the boil and add the cooked rice and the chicken meat to it. Allow to simmer for a few minutes. Add the black pepper and the nam pla. Take six individual soup bowls and break an egg into each one. Ladle the boiling soup onto the eggs. Garnish with the spring onion and the coriander leaves and serve immediately.

Serves 6

Thai Chicken and Mushroom Soup

An apparently ordinary soup with an extraordinary flavour typical of Thailand

2 lb (1 kg) uncooked chicken backs (carcass excluding legs and breasts) and
    giblets
2 spring onions, cut into 1 in (2.5 cm) strips
8 cups water

1 teaspoonful salt
8 dried mushrooms
4 cloves garlic, crushed
1 tablespoonful coriander root, when available
1 tablespoonful oil
¼ teaspoonful ground black pepper
1 tablespoonful fish sauce (nam pla)

Put the chicken, the spring onion, the water and salt into a large saucepan and bring to the boil. Cover and simmer for about 2 hours. Strain the chicken stock. Remove any chicken meat from the bones and reserve it. Soak the mushrooms in hot water for 30 minutes. Discard the tough stems of the mushrooms and slice into three. Using a mortar and pestle or an electric blender, grind the garlic and the coriander if available. Heat the oil in a pan, add the ground ingredients and stir fry for a minute or two. Add the chicken meat and stir. Add the pepper, the nam pla, the stock and the mushrooms and bring to the boil. Simmer for 5 minutes. Serve immediately.

Serves 4–6

Soto Ayam (1) (Indonesian Chicken Soup)

In Indonesia there are many ways of making what is basically a chicken soup. It can be simple, with only the addition of a few noodles, or it can be elaborate. When eaten with rice and garnished with hardboiled eggs and spring onions, it can be a meal in itself.

3 lb (1.3 kg) chicken, cut into quarters
3 pints (1.7 l) water
1 medium onion, chopped
a few celery stalks
2 cloves garlic, chopped
1 teaspoonful ginger, chopped
½ teaspoonful mace
1 teaspoonful whole peppercorns
1 teaspoonful salt
4 oz (113 g) noodles

Garnish
3 hardboiled eggs, chopped
3 spring onions, finely chopped

In a large pan bring the chicken to the boil in the cold water. Add the onion, celery stalks, garlic, ginger, mace, whole peppercorns and salt. Simmer for 1 hour. Strain the stock and reserve. Remove the skin and the bones from the chicken and cut the chicken meat into small pieces. Bring a pan of water to the boil, drop the noodles into it and cook according to the instructions on the packet. Reheat the chicken stock and chicken meat and add the cooked noodles to it. Bring to the boil. Garnish with the hardboiled eggs and spring onions and serve immediately.

Serves 4–6

Soto Ayam (2) (Indonesian Chicken Soup)

To serve this soup, place all the separate dishes of garnishes on the table with the soup in the centre. Each guest first helps himself to a small quantity of the garnishes and pours the hot soup over. Lime or lemon juice is added according to taste. Sometimes the rice and sambal are eaten separately.

3 lb (1.3 kg) chicken, cut into quarters
3 pints (1.7 l) cold water
1 medium onion, chopped
a few celery stalks
1 teaspoonful whole peppercorns
1 teaspoonful salt
3 tablespoonsful peanut oil
4 curry leaves, when available
1 medium onion, finely chopped
1 teaspoonful ginger, chopped
2 cloves garlic, chopped
2 red chillies, finely chopped
½ teaspoonful ground turmeric
1 tablespoonful ground coriander
1 teaspoonful ground cumin
½ teaspoonful ground fennel
½ teaspoonful ground mace

Garnish
3 hardboiled eggs, sliced
6 spring onions, finely sliced
1 packet potato crisps, roughly crumbled
4 oz (113 g) vermicelli, soaked in water for 15 minutes, drained, and fried until
  crisp
2 oz (56 g) bean sprouts, soaked in cold water and then immersed in boiling
  water for 1 minute

1 *bowl plain boiled rice*
sambal ulek (see RELISHES AND SAMBOLS*)*
lime or lemon wedges

In a large pan bring the chicken to the boil in the cold water. Add
the onion, celery, peppercorns and salt. Simmer for 1 hour. Strain
the stock and reserve. Remove the skin and bones from the chicken
and cut the meat into pieces. In a large pan heat the oil. Fry the
curry leaves, onions, ginger, garlic and chilli. Add the turmeric,
coriander, cumin, fennel and mace and fry for half a minute. Add
the chicken stock and chicken meat and simmer for 15 minutes.

Serves 6–8

Watercress Soup

This is a simple tasty soup which can be made easily once the basic
stock is ready.

4 oz (113 g) pork tenderloin
½ tablespoonful cornflour
4 oz (113 g) watercress
basic chicken stock (see BASIC RECIPES*)*
1 teaspoonful salt
1 tablespoonful soy sauce

Chop the pork very finely. Mix the cornflour with a tablespoonful of
cold water. Wash the watercress and discard any tough stems. In a
medium sized pan bring the stock to the boil. Add the salt, soy
sauce and pork and allow to simmer for 5 minutes. Add the
cornflour and stir constantly until the soup thickens. Lastly, add
the watercress and allow to boil for 2 minutes.

Serves 4

Sop Kangkung (Watercress Soup, Indonesian Style)

Kangkung is a leafy green vegetable that grows in abundance in
marshy low-lying areas. Watercress is a suitable substitute for this.

1 lb (454 g) watercress
4 oz (113 g) fillet of pork

½ teaspoonful brown sugar
1 teaspoonful cornflour
1 tablespoonful soy sauce
1½ tablespoonsful peanut oil
1 teaspoonful fresh ginger, grated
1 teaspoonful salt
½ teaspoonful ground black pepper
2 pints (1.2 l) boiling water

Wash and shred the watercress. Marinade the pork, cut in cubes, in the brown sugar, cornflour and soy sauce for 15 minutes. In a medium sized pan heat the oil and fry the ginger for a couple of seconds. Add the pork and the marinade, the salt and pepper. Add the boiling water to the pork. When the water returns to boiling point add the watercress and simmer for 20 minutes.

Serves 4–6

Velvet Corn Soup

A Chinese soup, easy to make and a good start to a Far Eastern meal.

1 chicken breast
2 egg whites
½ tablespoonful cornflour
2 slices smoked bacon or ham
basic chicken stock (see BASIC RECIPES)
1 × 8 oz (226 g) can creamed corn
½ teaspoonful salt

Remove the chicken flesh from the bone and chop very finely, using a sharp knife. Beat the egg whites in a bowl until frothy. Mix the cornflour with a tablespoonful of water. Cut the bacon or ham into small pieces. In a medium sized pan bring the chicken stock to the boil. Add the corn and chicken to it and allow to simmer for 3 minutes. Add the salt and the cornflour and boil on a high heat until the soup has thickened. Remove from heat and pour in the beaten egg white. Sprinkle in the ham or bacon. Stir the soup and serve immediately in individual bowls.

Serves 4

Sop Kembang Kol (Cauliflower Soup, Indonesian Style)

chicken stock (see recipe for Soto Ayam (1))
1 medium cauliflower, cut into small chunks
$\frac{1}{4}$ teaspoonful freshly ground black pepper
$\frac{1}{4}$ teaspoonful freshly ground nutmeg
4 oz (113 g) egg noodles
1 teaspoonful salt

Bring the chicken stock to the boil. Add the cauliflower, the spices and the noodles and boil for about 5 minutes. Care should be taken not to overcook the cauliflower and noodles. Serve immediately.

Serves 4–6

Bean Curd Soup

This could be a soup from one of several Far Eastern countries. This particular recipe, however, comes from Thailand.

8 oz (226 g) bean curd
2 oz (56 g) minced pork
$2\frac{1}{2}$ cups cold water
1 tablespoonful fish sauce (nam pla)
2 cloves garlic, crushed
1 teaspoonful salt
3 spring onions, cut into 1 in (2.5 cm) lengths
coriander leaves, for garnishing

Cut the bean curd into cubes. Put the minced pork and cold water in a pan and bring slowly to the boil. Add the bean curd and the nam pla, the garlic and salt, and simmer for 5 minutes. Add the spring onions and coriander leaves and serve immediately.

Serves 4

Miso Shiru

Perhaps the most popular of all Japanese soups, and quick and easy to prepare.

1 sachet (0.3 oz/9 g) dashinomoto
5 cups hot water
3 tablespoonsful red bean paste (aka-miso)

6 oz (168 g) bean curd (tofu)
3 spring onions, finely sliced

In a pan bring the dashinomoto and the hot water to the boil. In a bowl mix the red bean paste to a smooth diluted paste with some of the hot stock. Pour the bean paste liquid back into the saucepan and bring to the boil. Cut the pieces of bean curd into bite-sized cubes and carefully slide into the soup. Add the spring onions and allow to boil for half a minute. Remove from the heat and ladle the soup into bowls, taking care not to break the cubes of bean curd.

Serves 4

Sumashi-Jiru (Consomme with Bean Curd)

This clear Japanese soup can be made in a matter of minutes and is ideal on a cold winter's day.

1 sachet (0.3 oz/9 g) dashinomoto
4½ cups hot water
½ teaspoonful salt
1 dessertspoonful soy sauce
12 oz (340 g) bean curd (tofu)
3 spring onions

In a pan bring the dashinomoto and the water to the boil. Add the salt and the soy sauce. Cut the bean curd into 1 in (2.5 cm) cubes, and carefully slide into the bubbling broth. Reduce the heat and simmer for 5 minutes. Cut the spring onions into very fine slices and add to the broth. Remove from the heat and ladle into bowls, taking care not to break the cubes of bean curd.

Serves 4–6

Sop Tahu (Indonesian Bean Curd Soup)

chicken stock (see recipe for Soto Ayam (1)
8 oz (226 g) bean curd
¼ cup tender celery, chopped

Garnish
crisp fried onion flakes

Bring the stock to the boil. Cut the bean curd into bite-sized pieces. Add the bean curd and celery to the stock and simmer for 10 minutes. Serve hot, garnished with onion flakes.

Serves 4–6

Hot and Sour Soup

A nourishing and tasty Chinese soup.

4 oz (113 g) pork tenderloin
4 dried mushrooms
6 oz (168 g) bean curd
2 oz (56 g) canned bamboo shoots
½ tablespoonful cornflour
basic chicken stock (see BASIC RECIPES)
1 tablespoonful soy sauce
1 teaspoonful salt
½ tablespoonful white vinegar
¼ teaspoonful freshly milled pepper
1 egg, lightly beaten
2 teaspoonsful sesame oil
2 spring onions, finely sliced

Cut the pork into fine slices. Soak the mushrooms in hot water for 30 minutes. Discard the stems and slice the caps finely. Cut the bean curd into 1 in (2.5 cm) cubes. Slice the bamboo shoots finely. Mix the cornflour with a tablespoonful of cold water. In a medium sized pan bring the chicken stock to the boil. Add the pork, soy sauce, salt, vinegar and pepper. Simmer for 5 minutes. Add the bamboo shoots and bean curd. Add the cornflour and stir constantly until the soup has thickened slightly. Carefully pour in the beaten egg and turn off the heat. Add the sesame oil and spring onions and serve at once.

Serves 4

Egg Drop Soup

This is one of the best known Chinese soups, and it is very easy to make.

basic chicken stock (see BASIC RECIPES)
½ teaspoonful salt
½ tablespoonful cornflour

1 egg, lightly beaten
2 spring onions, finely sliced

Bring the chicken stock to the boil in a medium sized saucepan.
Mix the cornflour with a tablespoonful of water. Add the salt and
the cornflour to the bubbling stock and stir until the soup becomes
clear. Carefully pour the beaten egg into the stock and turn off the
heat. Divide the soup between four bowls, garnish with the sliced
spring onion and serve at once.

Serves 4

Kakitama-Jiru (Egg Drop Soup)

This soup is popular in both Japan and China. This is the Japanese
version: the dashinomoto adds a distinctive Japanese flavour.

1 sachet (0.3 oz/9 g) dashinomoto
4½ cups hot water
2 teaspoonsful cornflour
1 dessertspoonful soy sauce
1 teaspoonful salt
2 eggs, lightly beaten
2 spring onions, finely sliced

In a pan bring the dashinomoto and the water to the boil. Mix the
cornflour with the soy sauce and salt and add it to the soup. Allow
this stock to boil gently. Add the beaten eggs a little at a time in a
thread-like stream, while stirring the stock to keep the threads of
beaten egg floating on the surface. Ladle into four bowls and
garnish with the spring onions.

Serves 4

Chawan Mushi

This savoury steamed egg custard is the only Japanese soup that is
eaten with a spoon. If the fish stock and seafood in this recipe do
not appeal to you, replace them with chicken stock and a larger
quantity of chicken breast. Care should be taken in the cooking to
ensure that the custard is barely set and yellow in colour, without
any brown crust on the surface.

8 eggs
1 sachet (0.3 oz/9 g) dashinomoto
2 tablespoonsful sake
2 tablespoonsful soy sauce
2 teaspoonsful salt
8 large mushrooms
1 large chicken breast
8 slices kamaboku (fish sausage) (optional)
8 prawns or shrimps
1 small bunch watercress

In a large bowl lightly mix the eggs. Dissolve the dashinomoto in hot water and gradually mix it into the eggs. Add the sake, soy sauce and the salt. This egg mixture should not have any froth or bubbles. Wash the mushrooms, discard the stems and slice each mushroom into three. Remove the flesh from the chicken breast and slice it fairly thinly. Place the kamaboku slices in a heatproof bowl, pour on boiling water to cover and leave for 2 minutes. Drain away the water. Remove the heads, tails and shells from the prawns, de-vein them and slit each into two.

Divide the egg mixture equally between eight heatproof bowls or ramekin dishes. Put equal amounts of prawn, chicken, mushrooms and the kamaboku into each dish. Cover each dish with foil and tie with twine so that the foil lid is secure. Place in a large saucepan (or two saucepans if you do not have one large enough) and pour a sufficient amount of boiling water to come halfway up the sides of the bowls. Cover and simmer for 12 minutes. Remove the lids and carefully place on the surface one or two watercress leaves per bowl. Replace the lids and continue to steam for a further 10 minutes or so, or until the custard is barely set.

Serves 8

Nabeyaki Udon

This Japanese soup is a meal in itself and is very satisfying on a cold winter's day

1 lb (454 g) udon noodles
6 cups dashi
⅓ cup soy sauce
½ cup mirin
a pinch of MSG
6 dried mushrooms

6 oz (170 g) fish sausage (kamaboku)
1 chicken breast
4 spring onions, sliced diagonally
6 prawns, fried tempura style (see pp. 114–15)

Bring a large pan of water to the boil. Add the noodles and bring back to the boil. Add a cup of cold water and bring back to the boil again. Allow to boil rapidly until the noodles are just cooked. Do not overcook. Drain in a colander and rinse under running cold water. Allow to drain.

In a large saucepan bring the dashi, soy sauce, mirin and MSG to the boil. Soak the mushrooms in hot water for 45 minutes. Slice the fish sausage and cut the chicken into pieces large enough to be picked up with chopsticks. Add the chicken and the mushrooms to the simmering stock and allow to boil for 5 minutes. Add the noodles and the fish sausage, the spring onions and prawns, and bring to the boil. Serve piping hot in six large bowls.

Serves 6

Shark's Fin Soup

A Chinese speciality, commonly regarded as an essential item on a Chinese menu.

4 Chinese dried mushrooms
½ tablespoonful cornflour
1 chicken breast
1 can shark's fin
basic chicken stock (see BASIC RECIPES)
½ teaspoonful salt
1 tablespoonful soy sauce
3 spring onions, finely sliced

Soak the mushrooms in hot water for 30 minutes. Discard the stems and slice the mushroom caps very finely. Mix the cornflour with a tablespoonful of cold water. Remove the flesh from the chicken breast and slice it finely. Bring the contents of the can of shark's fin and the chicken stock to the boil in a medium sized pan. Add the salt, the soy sauce, the chicken and the mushrooms, and allow to simmer for 5 minutes. Add the cornflour and stir constantly until the soup has thickened slightly. Garnish with spring onions and serve immediately.

Serves 4

Sour Prawn Soup

A Thai speciality, this soup has an unusual hot and sour taste. If fresh prawns are available begin by making a stock using the washed prawn heads. But if frozen prawns have to be used, use water-based stock instead.

1½ lb (680 g) prawns, fresh or frozen
6 cups water
2 stalks lemon grass or 2 pieces lemon peel
2 lime or lemon leaves, if available
½ teaspoonful salt
3 whole fresh chillies
1 tablespoonful fish sauce (nam pla)
2 tablespoonsful lime or lemon juice
1 sprig coriander leaves
2 spring onions, finely chopped

If the prawns are fresh remove the heads and shell and de-vein them. Wash the prawns thoroughly. Bring six cups of stock made from the prawn heads and shells, or six cups of water to the boil in a pan. Add the lemon grass or lemon peel, the lime or lemon leaves, the salt and the chillies. Simmer for 15 minutes. Strain the liquid and bring back to the boil. Add the prawns, the fish sauce and the lime or lemon juice. Allow to simmer for 4 minutes. Serve hot, garnished with the coriander leaves and spring onion.

Serves 4–6

Wonton Soup

This is a substantial Chinese soup with an unusual flavour.

basic chicken stock (see BASIC RECIPES)
16 wontons (uncooked) (see recipe on pp. 175–6)
4 oz (113 g) watercress
2 teaspoonsful soy sauce

In a large pan bring 2 pints (1.2 litres) of water to the boil. Drop the wontons into the boiling water and allow to cook for 5–7 minutes. Drain away the water and reserve the wontons. In a medium sized pan bring the stock to the boil. Add the watercress, soy sauce, and wontons and allow to boil for 2 minutes. Serve at once.

Serves 4

Mulligatawny (Spiced Beef Broth)

A South Indian soup, also eaten by the Tamils in Sri Lanka.

1 lb (454 g) beef, cut into small pieces
1 lb (454 g) soup bones
2 medium onions, chopped
2 teaspoonsful fresh ginger, finely chopped
6 cloves garlic, finely chopped
¼ teaspoonful turmeric
1 teaspoonful cumin powder
2 teaspoonsful coriander powder
15 peppercorns
2–3 bay leaves
2 carrots, diced
1½ teaspoonsful salt
1 tablespoonful oil
1 onion, finely sliced
3 oz (85 g) creamed coconut
lime or lemon juice

Put the first twelve ingredients in a large pan, cover generously with cold water and bring to the boil. Simmer on a *very* low heat for about 2 hours. (Where a pressure cooker is available the cooking time of the stock is reduced to about 20 minutes.) Strain the stock carefully saving the carrots, the onions and the pieces of meat.

In another pan heat the tablespoonful of oil and lightly brown the finely sliced onion. Add the stock, meat and vegetables to the hot onion. Lastly add the creamed coconut and allow it to dissolve on a low heat in the soup. Prior to serving add a dash of lime or lemon juice (about 1 tablespoonful). Serve hot either as a soup or as a gravy with boiled rice.

Serves 4

2

Rice Dishes

Pilaf Rice

A delicately flavoured rice dish to be served with curries and accompaniments. An Indian speciality.

2 tablespoonsful butter, ghee or oil
1 medium onion, finely chopped
1 cup rice (washed in a sieve under running cold water and left to drain)
1 teaspoonful salt
6 cardamoms, 6 cloves and 1 in (2.5 cm) length stick cinnamon
a few curry leaves (optional)
1 chicken stock cube
2 cups water

Heat the fat in a saucepan and brown the onion in it. Add all the other ingredients (except the stock cube and water) and fry over a gentle heat for 5 minutes. Lastly add the water in which the stock cube has been dissolved and bring to a rapid boil. Stir, cover and simmer for 15 minutes.

As an optional variation, add 4 oz (113 g) finely sliced fried mushrooms for garnish.

Serves 3–4

Kiri Bath (Sri Lankan Coconut Milk Rice)

This is the most traditional of all Sri Lankan rice dishes, served on religious and national festival days. It is usually spread on a platter about 1 in (2.5 cm) deep, cut into diamond-shaped pieces and served with a hot onion sambal or jaggery.

2 cups rice
1 teaspoonful salt
3 cups water
3 oz (85 g) creamed coconut
2 cups boiling water

Put the rice, salt and three cups of water in a pan and bring to the boil. Cover, lower the heat and simmer for 10 minutes. Dissolve the creamed coconut in the two cups of boiling water. Add it to the rice. Stir the rice, cover and cook on a very low heat for about 10–12 minutes or until all the moisture is absorbed. Spread on a platter, cut into pieces and serve.

Serves 4–6

Kichiri

A nourishing and tasty Indian dish combining lentils and rice.

$\frac{1}{2}$ cup yellow moong dhal
$\frac{1}{2}$ cup rice
2 tablespoonsful oil
1 medium onion, sliced
$\frac{1}{2}$ teaspoonful salt
$\frac{1}{8}$ teaspoonful turmeric
2 cups hot water
$\frac{1}{2}$ teaspoonful cumin powder
$\frac{1}{2}$ teaspoonful coriander powder
$\frac{1}{4}$ teaspoonful mustard seed
a few curry leaves

Wash the lentils and soak them in water for 2 hours. Wash the rice
and drain lentils and rice in a sieve. Heat the oil and fry the onion
until lightly brown. Add the rice and lentils and fry over a low
heat for about 5 minutes. Add all the other ingredients and bring to
the boil. Cover and simmer for 15 minutes.

Serves 3–4

Nasi Gurih (Indonesian Coconut Rice)

8 oz (226 g) long grain rice
3 oz (85 g) creamed coconut
$2\frac{1}{2}$ cups of water
2–3 curry leaves, when available
1 piece of lemon grass or $\frac{1}{2}$ teaspoonful grated lime or lemon rind
1 teaspoonful salt

Wash the rice in a large sieve under running cold water until the
water that runs is clear. Allow the rice to drain. In a medium
sized pan over a low heat dissolve the creamed coconut in the
water. Add the curry leaves, lemon grass and salt. Lastly add the
rice and bring to the boil. Stir the rice, put the lid on and lower the
heat so as to just simmer. Allow to cook for 20 minutes.

Serves 4

Kaha Bath (Sri Lankan Yellow Rice)

Yellow rice is served at feasts and on festive occasions, usually with numerous accompaniments.

½ medium onion, finely chopped
2 tablespoonsful ghee, butter or oil
1 cup rice (washed in a sieve under running cold water and left to drain)
a few curry leaves
3 cloves
3 cardamoms
1 in (2.5 cm) stick cinnamon
1 teaspoonful salt
¼ teaspoonful saffron or turmeric
8 peppercorns
2 cups water in which 4 oz (113 g) creamed coconut has been dissolved

Fry the finely chopped onion in the oil. Add all the other dry ingredients and fry over a low heat until the grains of rice become pale brown. Add the coconut milk and bring to a rapid boil. Cover and simmer for 15 minutes.

Serves 3–4

Nasi Kuning (Indonesian Yellow Rice)

This is a rice dish made for festivals in Indonesia. The rice is garnished with meat balls (rempah), slices of hardboiled egg, cucumber, fried shrimps, crisp fried onions and strips of red chilli.

1 lb (454 g) long grain rice
6 oz (168 g) creamed coconut
2½ cups hot water
2–3 curry leaves, when available
1 piece lemon grass or ½ teaspoonful grated lime or lemon rind
2 strips pandams leaf, when available.
1½ teaspoonsful salt
1 teaspoonful ground turmeric

In a sieve, wash the rice under running cold water until the water runs clear. Allow to drain. In a medium sized pan over a low heat dissolve the creamed coconut in the hot water. Add the rice and the rest of the ingredients and bring rapidly to the boil. Put the lid on and turn the heat down so as just to simmer and allow to cook for about 10–15 minutes or until the water has evaporated. Put the rice into a bowl and cover the bowl securely. Put the bowl in a colander and steam, covered, over boiling water for about 20 minutes.

Garnish
½ cucumber, finely sliced
2 hardboiled eggs, cut into quarters
2 red chillies, de-seeded and cut into strips
1 medium onion, finely sliced and deep fried until golden brown
2 oz (56 g) shrimps, stir fried in 1 fl oz (28 ml) vegetable oil

Rempah (Meat Balls)
4 oz (113 g) desiccated coconut
8 oz (226 g) lean minced beef
1 clove garlic, finely chopped
½ medium onion, finely chopped
½ teaspoonful brown sugar
½ teaspoonful coriander powder
½ teaspoonful cumin powder
½ teaspoonful salt
1 egg, beaten
oil for deep frying

Soak the coconut in two tablespoonsful of hot water for 10 minutes. Mix all the ingredients, including the coconut, in a large bowl. Shape into small, bite-sized balls. Deep fry a few at a time until golden brown. Drain on kitchen paper. These meat balls can also be eaten cold or served with drinks.

Arrange the steamed rice on a platter and decorate with the sliced hardboiled eggs, fried onion, chilli, shrimps, cucumber and meat balls.

Serves 6–8

Chicken Biriani

This is an Indian rice preparation that is served at feasts. Ideal for a dinner party, served with pickle and chutney.

¼ teaspoonful cumin powder
¼ teaspoonful coriander powder
½ teaspoonful paprika
¼ teaspoonful turmeric
8 cloves
seeds of 8 cardamom pods

$\frac{1}{2}$ teaspoonful cinnamon
1 green chilli (optional)
1 medium onion
3 cloves garlic
1 teaspoonful ginger, finely chopped
$\frac{1}{2}$ teaspoonful tomato purée
1 teaspoonful salt
$\frac{1}{2}$ cup yoghurt
1 lb (454 g) fresh chicken meat, de-boned
2 tablespoonsful ghee, butter or oil
$\frac{1}{2}$ medium onion, finely chopped
$1\frac{1}{2}$ cups rice, washed and drained in a sieve
$1\frac{1}{2}$ cups hot water
1 chicken stock cube
$\frac{1}{2}$ teaspoonful salt
$\frac{1}{4}$ teaspoonful saffron

Garnish
2 oz (56 g) cashew nuts
8 oz (226 g) onions, finely sliced

Blend the first fourteen ingredients in a liquidizer. Cut the chicken into bite-sized pieces and marinade in the spicy yoghurt mixture for at least 4 hours.

Heat a tablespoonful of the oil and fry the onion until golden brown. Add the rice and fry over a low heat until the grains are transparent. Dissolve the stock cube in the water, add to the rice and bring to the boil, adding the salt. Cover and simmer for 10 minutes.

While the rice is cooking heat the remaining oil and quickly fry the chicken in it. Pour in the marinade and simmer for about 5 minutes.

Use a large casserole dish and place a third of the rice at the bottom. Put half the chicken over the rice and cover with a third of the rice. Put on the remainder of the chicken and cover with the rice. Measure the marinade liquid and if it is less than a cup add hot water to make it up. Dissolve the saffron in the marinade liquid and pour it over the casserole. Bake, covered, at Gas Mark 3/325°F for 45 minutes.

Garnish with fried cashew nuts and the onions which have been deep fried until golden brown.

Serves 4

Vegetable Biriani

This is a delicious vegetable rice dish, a recipe that is quite basic in an Indian culinary repertoire. Leftover cold meat may be added to make a nourishing 'all in one' dish.

1 cup rice (washed in a sieve under running cold water and left to drain)
2 cups water
1 teaspoonful salt
8 oz (226 g) aubergines
8 oz (226 g) onions
4 oz (113 g) green pepper, chopped
8 oz (226 g) firm ripe tomatoes, chopped
1 pint (568 ml) cooking oil for deep frying

Put the rice, water and salt in a pan and bring to the boil. Stir, cover and simmer for 15 minutes. While the rice is cooking cube and deep fry the aubergines. Finely slice the onions, fry until golden brown and leave to drain. Using a 4 pint (2.4 l) casserole assemble all the ingredients in layers, starting and finishing with the rice. Cover with a well-fitting lid and bake at Gas Mark 3/325°F for half an hour. (Half a pint (280 ml) of double cream poured over the top makes an interesting change.)

Serves 3–4

Nasi Goreng (Fried Rice)

One of the most popular Indonesian rice dishes in the West. It is an ideal way of using up leftover cold rice and when eaten with fried eggs is a quick, easy dish to prepare. It is sold everywhere in Indonesia by street vendors.

2 eggs
salt
oil for deep frying
1 large onion, finely sliced
½ cucumber, finely sliced
3 spring onions, finely sliced
8 oz (226 g) fillet steak, finely sliced
4 oz (113 g) prawns or shrimps, de-veined and cleaned
1 clove garlic
1 small onion, finely chopped
½ teaspoonful dried shrimp paste (trasi)
boiled rice (see BASIC RECIPES)
1 tablespoonful soy sauce

First prepare the garnishes. Beat the eggs and add a pinch of salt to them. Lightly grease a frying pan with a small quantity of oil and make two thin omelettes. Slice the omelettes and reserve. Deep fry the sliced onion over a medium heat until golden brown, taking care not to burn it. Finely slice the cucumber and the spring onion.

Heat a wok or large frying pan. Add a tablespoonful of oil to it, and when that is hot add the steak and prawns. Fry over a medium heat. Then add the garlic, the onion and the trasi which has been crushed. Stir fry for a couple of minutes. Finally add the rice and spring onions. Sprinkle the soy sauce over the rice and mix thoroughly over a low heat until everything is heated through. Pile the rice into a mound and garnish with the chopped omelettes, sliced cucumber and fried onion.

Serves 4

Khao Phat (Fried Rice)

Mixed fried rice is a popular dish in many Asian countries, and it is versatile in that any ingredients that are readily available can be tossed in with the rice. This particular recipe comes from Thailand.

2 tablespoonsful vegetable oil
1 medium onion, finely chopped
1 clove garlic, finely chopped
4 oz (113 g) fillet of pork, cut into bite-sized pieces
4 oz (113 g) prawns or shrimps, shelled and de-veined
2 eggs
salt and pepper to taste
3 cups cooked cold white rice (see BASIC RECIPES*)*
1 tablespoonful fish sauce
⅛ teaspoonful MSG
½ cup spring onions, finely chopped

Garnish
cucumber slices
coriander leaves
1 fresh red chilli

In a wok or large frying pan heat the oil over medium heat. Add the chopped onion and garlic and fry for a couple of minutes until the onions are softened in the oil. Add the pieces of pork and fry for about 3 minutes. Add the shrimps or prawns and continue to fry until they are cooked through. In a bowl beat the eggs and add salt and pepper to taste. Pour the beaten egg into the wok and when barely set add the rice and mix thoroughly. Continue to stir until all the ingredients are properly mixed. Add the fish sauce, the MSG and the spring onions and stir thoroughly. Pile the rice into four dishes and garnish with the cucumber, finely chopped coriander leaves and the red chilli.

Serves 4

Sushi

Rice seasoned with vinegar and sugar forms the basis of this popular and versatile Japanese lunchtime snack. The rice is encased in sheets of bean curd (Ihari Sushi) or rolled in fine sheets of seaweed (Norimaki Sushi) or forms the outer wrapping of raw fish (Nigiri Sushi) to provide a wide variety of delicious snacks.

Rice for sushi
2 cups short grain rice
2¼ cups cold water
3 tablespoonsful mild vinegar
1½ tablespoonsful sugar
1 teaspoonful salt
1 tablespoonful mirin (optional)

Place the rice in a sieve and wash under cold running water, until the water that runs is clear. Allow to drain for about half an hour. Put the rice and the water into a medium sized saucepan and bring rapidly to the boil. Reduce the heat so as to just simmer, put the lid on and cook for 15 minutes. Remove from the heat and allow to cool slightly without opening the lid. Mix together the vinegar, sugar, salt and mirin. Lightly fork the warm rice and put it into a large bowl. Pour the dressing over and fold it into the rice.

Chirashi Sushi

This can only be described as a Japanese mixed rice salad. It is versatile in that you can add whatever ingredients are readily available.

2 dried mushrooms
1 medium carrot

soy sauce
sugar
2 eggs
salt
2 oz (56 g) canned tuna fish
2 oz (56 g) fresh or frozen shrimps
a handful of cooked green peas
1 piece canned lotus root, finely sliced
2 cups sushi rice (see recipe above)
finely sliced pickled ginger (beni shoga) (optional)

Soak the mushrooms in hot water for about an hour until they are soft. Discard the stems and slice the caps finely. Finely slice the carrot and boil in salted water to which a tablespoonful of soy sauce and a pinch of sugar have been added. Drain and allow to cool. Beat the eggs, add a pinch of salt and make two paper-thin omelettes, taking care not to have any brown specks on them. Finely shred the omelettes. Drain the tuna fish and flake it. Cook the shrimps in boiling salted water and allow to drain. Set aside a small amount of peas, lotus root and omelette for garnishing. Combine the rest of the ingredients in a large bowl and mix thoroughly. Scatter the reserved garnishings as attractively as possible to give a colourful display and serve cold.

Serves 6

Norimaki Sushi

Seasoned Japanese rice, with vegetables, egg and fish, is rolled in a paper-fine sheet of seaweed and cut like a swiss roll. The visual impact of the dark green seaweed against the rice with its colourful fillings is effective. If the idea of raw fish does not appeal to you it can be omitted.

2 eggs
salt
½ small cucumber
2 dried mushrooms
1 teaspoonful horseradish (wasabi) powder
6 sheets nori (seaweed)
2 cups sushi rice (see recipe above)
2 oz (56 g) finely sliced fresh raw tuna (optional)

Beat the eggs and add a little salt and make two paper-fine omelettes. Cut the omelettes into thin strips. Wash and cut the cucumber into $\frac{1}{4}$ in (6 mm) strips. Soak the mushrooms in hot water for about an hour. When soft discard the stalks and finely slice the mushrooms into long pieces. Mix the horseradish with a little cold water to form a stiff paste. Place a sheet of nori on a bamboo mat or clean cloth. Spread a sixth of the sushi rice evenly over the sheet of nori. In the centre, across the length of the nori, arrange a strip of omelette, a length of cucumber and mushrooms, and raw tuna which has been dipped into the wasabi paste. This process is similar to that of making pin wheel sandwiches. Roll tightly into a cylindrical shape. Repeat the process until all the ingredients are used. Allow to rest for a quarter of an hour before removing the mat. Using a very sharp knife cut the sushi into fairly thick neat slices.

Serves 6

Nigiri Sushi

Seasoned balls of rice topped with raw or cooked fish is one of the most popular sushi dishes eaten throughout Japan.

1 dessertspoonful horseradish (wasabi) powder
12 oz (340 g) very fresh tuna or bream
2 cups sushi rice (see recipe above)
8 oz (226 g) very fresh squid
soy sauce
fresh ginger, finely sliced

Mix the horseradish with a little cold water to form a fairly stiff paste. Cut the fish into thin rectangular pieces, about $2 \times 1\frac{1}{4}$ in (5 × 4 cm). Wet your hands in cold water and take about two tablespoonsful of rice and mould into an oval shape. Lightly coat a piece of fish with the horseradish paste and press onto the rice. If the squid is very fresh it can be eaten raw or else it can be blanched by immersing in boiling salted water for 2 minutes. Cut the squid into rectangular pieces and proceed as with the fish. The rice balls are dipped into soy sauce and eaten with a thin slice of ginger.

Serves 4

Ihari Sushi

Another version of Japanese sushi: bags made of fried bean curd are filled with seasoned rice to make a tasty lunchtime snack.

6 sheets fried bean curd (aburagé)
1 tablespoonful sugar
2 tablespoonsful soy sauce
½ cup dashi
1 tablespoonful mirin
2 cups sushi rice (see recipe above)

Pour boiling water over the bean curd in order to remove some of the excess oil. In a pan bring the sugar, soy sauce, dashi and mirin to the boil. Cut each sheet of bean curd into two and pull apart from the centre to form a bag. Add these prepared bags to the boiling liquid. Reduce the heat and simmer in order to absorb most of the liquid. Remove from the heat and drain on kitchen paper until fairly dry. Fill the 'bags' with sushi rice and make a neat parcel by rolling the top. Serve with other varieties of sushi.

Serves 6

Kitsune Donburi

Kitsune is the Japanese word for fox and the dish is so named because of the animal's alleged partiality for bean curd. Donburi is Japanese for a china bowl and a varied range of Donburis are possible, depending on the ingredients that are available.

2 sheets fried bean curd (aburagé)
2 cups dashi or chicken stock
½ cup soy sauce
½ teaspoonful sugar
¾ cup mirin
pinch MSG
4 spring onions
2 cups cooked rice

Pour boiling water over the bean curd to remove some of the excess oil. Cut the bean curd into rectangular strips $2\frac{1}{2} \times 1\frac{1}{2}$ in (5×3.8 cm). In a saucepan boil the dashi or stock, soy sauce, sugar, mirin and MSG for about 5 minutes. Slice the spring onion into diagonal strips and add it to the simmering stock. Divide the rice into four large bowls. Ladle the hot broth over the rice.

Serves 4

3

Noodle Dishes

Burmese Mixed Noodles

This is a popular Burmese recipe that lends itself to many variations of the basic ingredients as available. Crabmeat, chicken livers or mushrooms may be used in place of prawns.

8 oz (226 g) fine cellophane noodles
2 fl oz (56 ml) vegetable oil
2 cloves garlic, crushed
10 spring onions, chopped
1 stick celery, chopped
2 oz (56 g) fresh spinach leaves or Chinese cabbage
4 oz (113 g) lean pork chops, de-boned and cubed
8 oz (226 g) de-boned chicken breasts, cut into cubes
8 oz (226 g) peeled prawns
1 teaspoonful salt
1 medium green pepper, finely sliced
2 tablespoonsful soy sauce

Cook the noodles following the instructions on the packet. Spread on a plate to cool and dry. In a wok heat the oil. Fry the garlic, onions, celery and the leaves for a few minutes. Stir in the pork, chicken and prawns and heat on a low flame until cooked. Add the salt, cooked noodles, green pepper and the soy sauce and stir over a low flame until heated through.

Serves 4

Bamie Goreng (Mixed Fried Noodles)

This Indonesian noodle dish is a complete meal in itself. It is versatile in that you can add whatever meat and vegetables are to hand. The success of the dish, however, depends on the vegetables being barely cooked so that they retain their crispness and colour. It is usually garnished with fried onion flakes, spring onions and slices of cucumber.

8 oz (226 g) egg noodles
1–2 tablespoonsful vegetable oil
2 cloves garlic, finely chopped
½ medium onion, finely chopped
4 oz (113 g) uncooked chicken flesh, cut into pieces
4 oz (113 g) prawns, shelled and de-veined
1 stick celery, finely chopped

$\frac{1}{2}$ teaspoonful salt
1 tablespoonful soy sauce
3 spring onions, sliced
$\frac{1}{2}$ cucumber, finely sliced
fried onion flakes

Cook the noodles according to the directions on the packet, making sure not to overcook them. Drain the noodles in a colander until needed. In a wok or large frying pan heat the oil. Add the garlic, onion, chicken and prawns and fry over a medium to high heat until the chicken and prawns are cooked. Add the celery and stir fry for a few seconds. Add the noodles and mix thoroughly. Lastly, add the soy sauce and salt and cook for a further minute or so until the dish is heated through. Serve in four shallow bowls and garnish with spring onions, cucumber and fried onion flakes.

Serves 4

Cha-chiang-mein (Boiled Egg Noodles with Meat Sauce)

A popular Chinese noodle dish.

1 lb (454 g) Chinese egg noodles
3 tablespoonsful vegetable oil
1 lb (454 g) de-boned pork shoulder, freshly minced
2 tablespoonsful Chinese rice wine, or pale dry sherry
1 teaspoonful sugar
2 tablespoonsful soy sauce
8 spring onions, finely shredded
6 tablespoonsful chicken stock
1 medium cucumber
5 cloves garlic, finely chopped

Cook the noodles according to the directions on the packet and set aside. In a wok heat half the oil until it just begins to smoke. Add the minced pork and stir fry until it browns lightly. Add the wine, sugar, soy sauce and half of the shredded onion and stir thoroughly. Then pour in the chicken stock and cook rapidly over a medium heat until all the stock has evaporated. Turn off the heat and cover to retain heat.

Cut the cucumber lengthwise in two and scoop out the seeds. Now cut into $\frac{1}{8}$ in (3mm) wide slices lengthwise, and each slice into 2 in (5 cm) lengths. Arrange the cucumber, garlic and the remaining onion on a platter. Place the cooked noodles in a deep serving bowl and toss quickly with the remainder of the oil. Now pour the hot meat sauce into a third serving bowl. Serve the noodles, the cucumber garnish and the meat sauce in the three separate serving dishes, combining as required at the table.

Serves 4

Zaru Soba

The Japanese answer to take-away fish and chips! These chilled noodles are extremely popular in the hot summer months and are very easy to prepare. Each guest simply dips his portion of noodles into the bowl of seasoned sauce before eating it.

12 oz (340 g) soba noodles
2 sheets seaweed (nori)
3 spring onions, finely sliced
1 tablespoonful fresh ginger, finely grated

Sauce
3 cups dashi
½ cup mirin
¾ cup soy sauce
salt and sugar to taste

In a large pan bring about 3 pints (1.7 l) of water to the boil. Add the noodles and bring rapidly back to the boil. Add a cup of cold water and bring to the boil again, cooking for about 1½ minutes or until the noodles are just cooked. Do not overcook. Drain immediately in a colander and rinse under running cold water. Then allow to drain thoroughly, until all the water has dripped away.

Dry roast the sheets of seaweed over a naked flame until crisp taking care to move the sheets over the flame so that they do not burn. Put the noodles onto six plates and crumble a little seaweed on top of them. Bring the sauce ingredients to the boil and allow to cool. Check for seasoning, adding salt and sugar to taste. Give each guest half a bowl of the sauce, to which he adds a little ginger and spring onions according to taste.

Serves 6

Mi Krob (Crisp Fried Rice Sticks)

This is a Thai speciality, an excellent all-in-one dish for a dinner party.

vegetable oil for frying
8 oz (226 g) rice sticks (available at Indian or Chinese stores)
1 medium onion, finely chopped
3 cloves garlic, finely chopped
4 oz (113 g) fillet of pork, cut into small pieces
4 oz (113 g) breast of chicken, cut into small pieces
4 oz (113 g) shrimps or prawns, washed and de-veined
4 oz (113 g) bean curd, finely chopped
10 spring onions, cut into pieces
1 tablespoonful lemon juice
2 tablespoonsful vinegar
2 tablespoonsful fish sauce (nam pla)
1 tablespoonful sugar
2 tablespoonsful coriander leaves, chopped
a handful of red chillies, sliced (optional)
1 oz (28 g) bean sprouts, washed

Heat a large quantity of oil and deep fry the rice sticks, a few at a time, on a medium to high heat until golden brown. Allow to drain on kitchen paper. In another wok heat four tablespoonsful of oil. Fry the onion and the garlic until evenly browned. Add the pork, chicken and shrimps and stir fry until they are cooked. Add the bean curd, spring onions, lemon juice, vinegar, fish sauce and sugar. Mix thoroughly. Lastly add the fried rice sticks and stir. Serve on four large platters, garnished with coriander leaves, chilli and bean sprouts.

Serves 4

Phat Wun Sen (Mixed Fried Rice Sticks)

A delicious rice stick preparation from Thailand.

8 oz (226 g) rice sticks (available at Indian or Chinese stores)
8 dried Chinese mushrooms
2 tablespoonsful oil
2 cloves garlic, finely chopped
4 oz (113 g) each fillet of pork and prawns (or shrimps)
1 carrot, cut into matchsticks
6 spring onions, cut into 1 in (2.5 cm) lengths

2 tablespoonsful fish sauce (nam pla)
1 tablespoonful vinegar
½ teaspoonful salt
¼ teaspoonful black pepper
1 teaspoonful sugar
coriander leaves for garnishing

Soak the rice sticks in hot water for 8–10 minutes and drain well. Soak the mushrooms in hot water for 15 minutes, drain away the water, discard the stems and finely slice the caps of the mushrooms. Heat the oil in a wok or large frying pan. Fry the garlic until light brown. Add the sliced pork and stir fry for 2 minutes. Add the prawns and cook for a further 2 minutes. Add the carrot, spring onions, mushrooms, fish sauce, vinegar, salt, pepper and sugar and mix thoroughly. Lastly, add the rice sticks and stir over a low heat until thoroughly mixed and heated through. Serve on a large platter and garnish with coriander leaves.

Serves 4

String Hopper Pilau (Savoury Rice Sticks)

Rice sticks are eaten in Sri Lankan homes several times a week. They are called 'string hoppers' and are freshly made each time with roasted rice flour. Commercially manufactured rice sticks are not normally used but they can be used effectively in this recipe to simulate a favourite Sri Lankan dish. They can be bought at Indian or Chinese grocery stores.

8 oz (226 g) rice sticks
2 tablespoonsful oil
½ medium onion, chopped
2 carrots, grated
½ cup fresh or frozen peas
½ green pepper, chopped
2 tablespoonsful tomato ketchup
1 teaspoonful salt
2 tablespoonsful water

In a large pan bring 2 pints (1.2 l) of water to the boil. Add the rice sticks, bring rapidly back to the boil and boil for 5 minutes. Drain in a colander. Heat the oil and fry the onion in it. Add the carrots, peas, green pepper, ketchup and salt and fry for 2 minutes. Add the water and simmer on a very low heat for 5 minutes. Stir in the rice sticks and mix thoroughly.

Serves 4

Mie Siam

This is a Thai version of a traditional Chinese dish.

8 oz (226 g) rice vermicelli
vegetable oil for deep frying
4 cloves garlic, chopped
2 spring onions, chopped
2 oz (56 g) each of pork, chicken and crabmeat
2 oz (56 g) prawns or shrimps
4 oz (113 g) bean curd, cut into bite-sized cubes
1 tablespoonful soy sauce
1 tablespoonful fish sauce (nam pla)
½ tablespoonful lime juice
¼ teaspoonful salt
2 teaspoonsful sugar
2 eggs, lightly beaten
4 oz (113 g) bean sprouts

Garnish
2 red chillies, de-seeded and cut into fine slices
a few coriander leaves and chives if available

Drop the vermicelli into boiling water and drain immediately in a colander. Spread thinly on a tea towel and leave until the water has evaporated. Heat the oil in a wok or deep frying pan until it is hot. Fry small quantities of the vermicelli until golden brown. Drain on kitchen paper. In a wok or large frying pan heat four tablespoonsful of oil. Add the garlic, spring onions, pork, chicken, crabmeat and prawns and stir fry until cooked. Add the bean curd, soy sauce, nam pla, lime juice, salt and sugar. Add the eggs and stir until well mixed. Add the fried vermicelli and bean sprouts and stir until heated through. Serve on a platter garnished with chillies, coriander leaves and chives.

Serves 4

Fried Beehoon

This mixed fried rice noodle dish is yet another that can be made with whatever meat and vegetables are available. If rice noodles are hard to come by use any other noodles that are available.

8 oz (226 g) rice sticks or noodles
3 tablespoonsful vegetable oil
2 oz (56 g) lean pork, chopped
4 oz (113 g) shrimps, fresh or frozen
3 cloves garlic, finely chopped
4 oz (113 g) bean sprouts
3 spring onions, cut into 1 in (2.5 cm) lengths
½ teaspoonful salt
1 tablespoonful soy sauce

Cook the noodles according to the directions on the packet and drain in a colander. In a wok heat the oil until it is smoking hot. Add the pork, shrimps and garlic and stir fry until the pork and shrimps are cooked. Add the bean sprouts, spring onions, salt and noodles and stir until thoroughly mixed. Add the soy sauce and continue to cook until the noodles are heated. Serve hot.

Serves 4

Orem Orem Istimewa

These steamed noodle packs are ideal for a picnic or for a sit-down Indonesian-style meal. In Indonesia the wrapping used is not tin foil but steamed banana leaves.

1 lb (454 g) egg noodles
7 oz (198 g) creamed coconut
1½ cups hot water
6 eggs
1½ teaspoonsful salt
¼ teaspoonful freshly milled pepper
a pinch of MSG *(optional)*
8 oz (226 g) minced beef
3 spring onions, finely sliced
12 tin foil squares (12 in/30 cm)

Cook the noodles according to the directions on the packet. Drain and allow to cool. Dissolve the creamed coconut in the hot water. Beat three eggs and mix into the creamed coconut. Add the seasonings. Mix the noodles into the seasoned creamed coconut. In another bowl mix together the remaining eggs, the meat and the spring onions. Divide the noodle mixture into twelve equal portions and place a portion on each of the tin foil sheets. Place equal portions of the minced meat over the noodles and wrap securely into neat parcels. Steam in a colander over rapidly boiling water for 45 minutes. Serve garnished with sliced tomatoes with ketchup or chilli sauce.

Serves 4

Laksa

This Malaysian speciality can be described as a rich soup consisting of noodles, seafood and vegetables in a coconut milk base. It is a meal in itself and well worth the effort!

8 oz (226 g) white fish fillets
½ teaspoonful salt
a pinch of freshly milled pepper
½ teaspoonful MSG
8 oz (226 g) prawns
6 oz (168 g) rice vermicelli
6 oz (168 g) bean sprouts
2 oz (56 g) crabmeat
1 cucumber, finely sliced
4 spring onions, finely sliced

Remove the fish skin and bones, if any, and mince the fish. In a bowl mix together the minced fish, salt, pepper and MSG. Shape into balls of a diameter of approximately 1 in (2.5 cm). Shell and de-vein the prawns. Soak the vermicelli in boiling water for 5 minutes and drain. Blanch the bean sprouts by immersing in boiling water for 1 minute and then drain in a colander. Run cold water over the bean sprouts. In a pan bring six cups of water to the boil. Carefully put the fish balls into the water, allow to simmer for 2 minutes, remove and add the prawns to the stock. Allow to simmer for 2 minutes and reserve.

Soup
2 tablespoonsful oil
1 small onion, finely chopped
2 cloves garlic, chopped
1 stalk lemon grass or ½ teaspoonful grated lemon rind

4 dried chillies, ground
1 teaspoonful blachan
1 teaspoonful turmeric
3 tablespoonsful coriander
4 oz (113 g) creamed coconut
1½ teaspoonsful sugar
1½ teaspoonsful salt
lime or lemon wedges for garnish

Heat the oil and fry the onion until golden brown. Add the garlic, lemon grass, chillies, blachan, turmeric and coriander. Now add the stock in which the fish and prawns were boiled. Add the creamed coconut, sugar and salt and bring to the boil. Simmer for 5 minutes. To serve divide the fish balls, vermicelli, prawns, crab, bean sprouts, cucumber and spring onions into six large soup bowls. Pour the steaming hot soup over it. Garnish with lime or lemon wedges.

Serves 6

4

Miscellaneous
Staples

Chappatis (Indian Bread)

Serve with vegetables or meat. Chappatis can be substituted for bread.

1 cup wholewheat flour
1 cup plain white flour
1½ teaspoonsful salt
5–6 fl oz (142–170 ml) tepid water

In a bowl mix the flours, salt, oil and sufficient water to form a soft pliable dough. Knead the dough thoroughly and leave, covered, at room temperature for about 1 hour. Divide the dough into ten equal portions, dust each portion generously with flour and roll out evenly to resemble a pancake.

Heat a griddle or a heavy bottomed frying pan. Turn the grill on to maximum. Place the pancake of dough on the griddle and cook for 4 seconds. Turn over and allow to cook for 8 seconds, or until the chappati is lightly brown. Now place the chappati on the grill (the browned side should be at the bottom). The chappati should puff up like a balloon. Prick with a fork to expel the hot air. Place on a plate and smear with butter or ghee.

Repeat the process until all the chappatis are made. Chappatis should be cooked quickly on a fairly high heat, otherwise they tend to become hard and leathery.

Serves 3–4

Puri

Deep fried Indian wholewheat bread. Puris are usually eaten with vegetables at the start of a meal and are a great favourite with both children and adults.

1 cup wholewheat flour
1 cup plain white flour
1½ teaspoonsful salt
5–6 fl oz (142–170 ml) tepid water
2 teaspoonsful oil
oil for deep frying

In a bowl mix the flours, oil and sufficient water to form a soft pliable dough. Knead the dough thoroughly and leave, covered, at room temperature for about an hour. A quantity of dough the size and shape of a walnut is rolled to resemble a thin pancake about 2½–3 in (6–8 cm) in diameter. This flattened dough is then deep fried. Since it requires much skill to make individual puris of perfect shape, I prefer to roll out one-third of the mixed dough at a time into a large thin pancake which is then cut into circles of about 2½–3 in (6–8 cm) diameter. A pastry cutter or wine glass is ideal.

The success of a puri is in its cooking. The oil should be heated until it begins to smoke, and the puris should be carefully immersed one at a time. After about 6 seconds in the hot oil the puri will begin to surface. Using a frying spoon gently pat it down to keep it submerged in the hot oil until it puffs up. Turn over and allow to cook for a couple of seconds. The whole frying process should take only about 15–20 seconds per puri.

Makes about 50, serves 6–8

Paratha

One of several bread substitutes used in India. Serve with vegetables or meat.

1 cup wholewheat flour
1 cup plain white flour
1½ teaspoonsful salt
5–6 fl oz (142–170 ml) tepid water
oil for shallow frying

In a bowl mix the flours, salt and sufficient water to form a soft pliable dough. Knead the dough thoroughly and leave, covered, at room temperature for about 1 hour. Divide the dough into ten equal portions. Roll each portion of dough to resemble a fine pancake. Using a pastry brush or the tips of your fingers rub some oil or ghee on half the circular area and fold over. Rub oil again on half the area and fold over once more. Now you should have a piece of dough resembling a quarter of a circle or quadrant. Roll out the quadrant again to resemble a pancake. Heat a tablespoon of oil or ghee in a frying pan. Shallow fry each quadrant for about 4 minutes on each side, adding more oil as necessary.

Serves 4

Upama (Savoury Semolina)

This is a South Indian breakfast dish but is equally nice eaten as a snack or with a curry for a main meal.

1¾ cups coarse semolina
1 tablespoonful oil
1 medium onion, finely chopped
½ teaspoonful cumin seeds
¼ teaspoonful turmeric powder
1 teaspoonful ginger, finely chopped
a few curry leaves (optional)
2 green chillies (optional)
2 carrots, grated
1 cup fresh or frozen peas
2 tomatoes, skinned and chopped
1 teaspoonful salt
2½ cups water
a handful of cashew nuts
a knob of butter

Roast the semolina in a heavy bottomed pan on a low heat, stirring constantly to prevent it from burning. In another pan heat the oil and fry the onions until they are golden brown. Add the cumin seeds, turmeric, ginger, curry leaves and green chillies. Add the vegetables, salt and water and bring to the boil. Lower the heat and allow to simmer for 10 minutes. Add the roasted semolina and stir over the lowest possible heat for 3–5 minutes. Remove from the heat and cover, leaving for 5 minutes. Add the cashew nuts and the knob of butter. Serve with pickle.

Serves 4–6

Roti Djala

These Indonesian pancakes should have a lacy appearance. They are made by dipping five fingers into the batter and allowing the mixture to drip into a hot frying pan. However, since this is a messy process drip the batter from a spoon or ladle, making an uneven movement to give the lacy look. Serve with dry meat curries.

8 oz (226 g) plain white flour
a pinch of salt
2 eggs, beaten

1½ cups water or milk

Mix the flour and salt in a bowl. Make a well in the centre and add the eggs and water or milk to form a thin smooth batter. Heat a frying pan and lightly grease it. Quickly spoon over small quantities of the batter in an uneven movement to form a perforated appearance. Turn over and cook for a couple of seconds. Repeat the process until all the batter is used up.

Serves 4–6

Lontong (Rice Cake)

An Indonesian speciality. Rice is encased in banana leaves and cooked in boiling water until it resembles a firm cake. The rice cake is sliced and used as an accompaniment to sates, and is sometimes used in soups. When banana leaves are unobtainable small muslin bags can be used instead.

8 oz (226 g) rice
¼ teaspoonful salt
4 muslin bags measuring 2 × 1½ in (5 × 3.8 cm)

Fill the bags with the rice and salt and sew up the open side. Place the bags in a pan containing boiling water and cook for about 2 hours. Snip open the bags and slice the rice cake.

Serves 4

Kachoori (Stuffed Deep Fried Dough)

This stuffed Indian bread is delicious with chutney or a vegetable curry.

Filling
½ cup split white urad dhal
1 tablespoonful oil
1 teaspoonful cumin seeds
3 green chillies, chopped
¼ teaspoonful turmeric
¼ teaspoonful asafoetida
½ teaspoonful salt
1 teaspoonful fresh ginger, finely chopped

Wash the dhal thoroughly and soak it overnight in a cup of cold water. Pour the dhal and the water into a liquidizer for a short time until the mixture is coarsely ground. In a pan heat the oil and add the cumin seeds to it. Once the seeds have sputtered add the chillies, turmeric, asafoetida, salt and ginger. Lastly add the ground dhal and cook over a low heat, stirring constantly until the water has evaporated. Spread out on a plate and allow to get cold.

Dough
1 cup plain white flour
1 cup wholewheat flour
1½ teaspoonsful salt
2 teaspoonsful oil
5–6 fl oz (142–170 ml) tepid water
oil for deep frying

In a bowl mix the flours, salt, oil and sufficient water to form a soft pliable dough. Knead the dough thoroughly and leave, covered, at room temperature for about an hour. Take a piece of dough about the size of a large walnut and flatten it in the palm of your hand. Place a small quantity of the filling (about half a teaspoonful) in the centre of the dough. Pinch the edges to seal securely. Flatten the dough again so that it resembles a small circular disc. Roll out on a floured board, taking care to apply gentle pressure on the rolling pin so that the filling does not ooze out. Heat the oil and fry one at a time as for puris (see recipe above).

Makes about 40, serves 6–8

Dosa (Lentil Pancakes)

A staple diet of the Tamils in South India and Sri Lanka. Serve with chutneys and vegetable curries.

1 cup split white urad dhal
2 cups rice
3 teaspoonsful salt

Wash the lentils in a sieve until the water that runs is clear. Soak overnight in two cups of water. Wash the rice thoroughly and soak overnight in three cups of water. Drain the lentils and rice. Grind the lentils to a smooth paste with a quarter cup of water. Grind the rice separately in a half cup of water. Mix the ground lentils and rice in a bowl and leave in a warm place for 36 hours. The mixture should now be fermented and frothy.

Heat a griddle or a heavy bottomed frying pan. Lightly grease the surface with a teaspoonful of oil. Pour in two tablespoonsful of the dosa mixture and, using the back of a metal knife, spread evenly over the surface of the pan. Pour a half teaspoonful oil round the circumference of the dosa. Using a spatula turn over and allow to brown lightly. Repeat the cooking process until all the batter is used.

Makes about 25, serves 6

5

Poultry Dishes

Indonesian Grilled Chicken

This is an Indonesian speciality – barbecued chicken liberally laced with pepper and red chilli – ideal for those who like hot food.

1 × 4 lb (2 kg) chicken
4 tablespoonsful soy sauce
4 tablespoonsful cooking oil
4 cloves garlic
2 teaspoonsful black pepper
1 teaspoonful coriander seed
10 dried red chillies
10 shallots

Cut the chicken into quarters. Grind the rest of the ingredients in a blender. Prick the chicken all over with a fork and marinade in the ground ingredients for 4 hours. Barbecue or grill on a low heat until the meat is cooked.

Serves 4

Sieu Ghuy (Chinese Barbecued Chicken)

In China numerous folk tales and superstitions are woven around poultry. The fowl represents many virtues, and chicken dishes are an undisputed delicacy.

1 × 3½ lb (1.5 kg) fresh chicken
4 tablespoonsful soy sauce
2 teaspoonsful sugar
1 clove garlic, finely chopped
1 teaspoonful ginger, finely chopped
1 teaspoonful 'five spices' (available at Chinese stores)
½ teaspoonful salt

Cut the chicken into joints. Mix the other ingredients in a bowl and marinade the chicken for about 1 hour. Cook the chicken pieces on a medium-hot grill, basting several times with the marinade. When the chicken is well roasted slice-chop Chinese-style into thin pieces about 3 in (6 cm) long and 1 in (2 cm) wide.

Serves 4

Chicken with Chestnuts

The chicken and chestnuts give a nicely contrasting texture in this Chinese speciality. If fresh chestnuts are used blanch for 15 minutes before adding to the chicken.

3 tablespoonsful dry sherry
3 tablespoonsful soy sauce
1 teaspoonful sugar
1 teaspoonful salt
2 tablespoonsful sesame oil
1 × 3½ lb (1.5 kg) chicken, de-boned and cut into bite-sized pieces
1 lb (454 g) chestnuts
2 teaspoonsful ginger, chopped
4 scallions

Mix the sherry, soy sauce, sugar and salt in a bowl. Add the chicken and allow to marinade for half an hour. In a shallow pan heat the oil and fry the chicken in it. Add the ginger, scallions and the marinade mixture and bring to the boil. Simmer for 15 minutes. If canned chestnuts are used drain away the water. Add the chestnuts to the chicken for the last 5 minutes of cooking.

Serves 4

Chicken Curry

This Indian chicken curry is spicy and the yoghurt adds an interesting tang to the flavour. Where time is limited powdered cumin and coriander can be used. The peppercorns, cardamoms, cloves and cinnamon can be replaced by 1½ teaspoonsful garam masala.

2 tablespoonsful oil
1 large onion, finely sliced
1 teaspoonful chilli powder
¼ teaspoonful turmeric
4 cloves garlic, crushed
1 teaspoonful fresh ginger, finely chopped
a few curry leaves (optional)
1 tablespoonful coriander
1 tablespoonful cumin
6 peppercorns
4 cloves
3 cardamoms

in (2.5 cm) piece of cinnamon
1½ teaspoonsful salt
4 chicken quarters, weighing approximately 3 lb (1.3 kg)
5 fl oz (142 ml) natural unsweetened yoghurt
2 fl oz (56 ml) water

Heat the oil. Fry the onions until golden brown. Add all the spices
and fry for a few minutes. Cool and grind in a blender. Heat
another tablespoonful of oil and gently fry the pieces of chicken.
Add the ground spices, the yoghurt and the water and simmer over
a low heat for about 45 minutes.

Serves 4

Kukul Mas Curry (Sri Lankan Chicken Curry)

This is a Sri Lankan party favourite, with the coconut adding a
distinctive flavour. It is usually eaten with a lot of chilli added to it,
but this could be varied to suit individual tastes.

2 large onions
2 tablespoonsful coriander powder
2 teaspoonsful cumin powder
½ teaspoonful turmeric
1 teaspoonful chilli powder
2 in (5 cm) stick cinnamon
¼ teaspoonful cardamom powder
5 cloves
½ teaspoonful green ginger, crushed
4 cloves garlic, finely chopped
2 teaspoonsful salt
4 fl oz (113 ml) vegetable oil
1 × 3 lb (1.3 kg) chicken, jointed
2 oz (56 g) creamed coconut
1½ cups hot water
juice of 1 lemon
2 tablespoonsful coriander leaves, finely chopped

Grind one of the onions, and the spices and salt. Finely slice the
second onion and fry in the heated oil until golden brown. Add the
ground ingredients and stir for 5–10 minutes. Now add the chicken
and fry for another 5 minutes. Dissolve the creamed coconut in the
hot water and add to the chicken. Bring to the boil, lower the heat
and simmer for about an hour. Before serving add the lemon juice
and garnish with the coriander leaves when available.

Serves 4

Burmese Chicken Curry

This Burmese delicacy is certainly for those who like it hot.

1 × 3½ lb (1.5 kg) chicken
1 teaspoonful turmeric
1 teaspoonful cumin powder
1 teaspoonful coriander powder
½ teaspoonful cinnamon powder
3 curry leaves (when available)
1 teaspoonful salt
2 tablespoonsful soy sauce
3 tablespoonsful sesame oil
1 medium onion, finely chopped
3 cloves garlic, finely chopped
4 dried chillies, finely chopped
2 cups water

Cut the chicken into joints. Mix together the spices and the soy sauce. Using a fork prick the chicken all over and marinade in the soy sauce and spices for 1 hour. Heat the oil and fry the onions until brown. Add the garlic and chillies. Then add the chicken and continue to fry for 10 minutes. Add the water and the marinade liquid and bring to a boil, then cover and simmer on a very low heat for about 1½ hours.

Serves 4

Opor Ayam

Chicken curry, Indonesian style.

1 × 3 lb (1.3 kg) fresh chicken
3 cloves garlic
1 teaspoonful fresh ginger, grated
2 teaspoonsful ground coriander
1 teaspoonful ground cumin
1 teaspoonful ground fennel
¼ teaspoonful ground black pepper
¼ teaspoonful ground cinnamon
3 tablespoonsful peanut oil
1 medium onion, finely sliced
½ cup hot water
a few curry leaves, if available
1 stalk lemon grass or ½ teaspoonful grated lemon rind

1¼ teaspoonsful salt
3 oz (84 g) creamed coconut
juice of ½ lemon

Cut the chicken into serving pieces. In a blender grind together the garlic, ginger, coriander, cumin, fennel, black pepper and cinnamon. Rub the ground ingredients on the chicken and allow to stand for half an hour. Heat the oil in a pan and fry the onions until they are soft. Add the chicken pieces and stir everything over a medium heat until well mixed. Now add the hot water, curry leaves, lemon grass and salt. Bring to the boil and allow to simmer over a low heat for about half an hour. Dissolve the creamed coconut in a quarter cup of boiling water. Add it and the salt to the chicken and continue to cook for a further half hour or until the chicken is cooked. Add the lemon juice and serve with boiled rice.

Serves 4

Ayam Kuning

A delicious dry chicken curry from Indonesia.

1 × 3 lb (1.3 kg) chicken
1½ teaspoonsful coriander seeds
1 teaspoonful cumin seeds
¾ teaspoonful turmeric
10 black peppercorns
4 cloves
3 cloves garlic
1 teaspoonful fresh ginger, grated
1 medium onion, chopped
10 macadamia nuts or whole almonds
2 tablespoonsful oil
a few curry leaves, when available
1½ teaspoonsful salt
¾ cup boiling water
3 oz (84 g) creamed coconut

Wash and cut the chicken into pieces. Grind the spices in a blender. Add the garlic, ginger, onion and nuts and grind to a smooth paste. In a pan heat the oil and fry the ground ingredients. Add the chicken and fry for about 5 minutes. Add the curry leaves, salt and boiling water, and bring to the boil. Cover and simmer for 45 minutes. Dissolve the creamed coconut in a quarter cup of boiling water, add to the chicken and simmer, uncovered, until all the liquid has evaporated.

Serves 4

Chicken Korma

This is a popular and well-known Indian dish which is not too spicy.

2 green chillies
1 teaspoonful fresh ginger, chopped
4 cloves garlic, chopped
6 cardamoms
6 peppercorns
½ teaspoonful ground cinnamon
2 dessertspoonsful desiccated coconut
2 dessertspoonsful ground coriander
1½ teaspoonsful salt
3 tablespoonsful oil
1 medium onion, sliced
4 chicken quarters, each cut into two
5 fl oz (142 ml) natural unsweetened yoghurt
½ chicken stock cube dissolved in 5 fl oz (142 ml) water
1 tablespoonful lemon juice

Using a blender or a pestle and mortar, grind together the first nine ingredients. Heat the oil and fry the sliced onion until brown. Remove the onions and fry the pieces of chicken in the same oil until lightly browned. Add the onion and the ground spices and stir for about 5 minutes. Add the yoghurt and stock and bring to the boil. Cover and simmer for about 1 hour. Before serving add the lemon juice and mix well.

Serves 2–3

Chicken Kashmiri-style

This is an interesting Kashmiri speciality combining a rich variety of exotic flavours.

1 fresh chicken, approximately 3½ lb (1.5 kg) in weight
2 tablespoonsful ghee or oil
1 medium onion, finely chopped

1 teaspoonful ginger, finely chopped
4 cloves garlic, finely chopped
½ teaspoonful salt
½ teaspoonful cinnamon powder
½ teaspoonful coriander powder
½ teaspoonful cumin powder
¼ teaspoonful freshly milled black pepper
½ teaspoonful ground cloves
½ teaspoonful cardamom powder
½ cup water
1 chicken stock cube
½ cup ground almonds
½ cup ground pistachio nuts
1 cup yoghurt
½ teaspoonful saffron powder

Remove the skin from the chicken. Using a sharp knife cut away as much of the flesh as possible from the carcass, cutting the chicken into convenient sized pieces. In a pan heat the oil and fry the onion until it is golden brown. Add the ginger, garlic and pieces of chicken and fry rapidly for about 5 minutes. Add the spices, water and chicken stock cube and simmer for about half an hour. Blend the ground nuts with the yoghurt. Mix the saffron with a teaspoonful of hot water. Add the yoghurt and saffron and bring to the boil. Simmer for 10 minutes before serving.

Serves 4

Tandouri Chicken

This most famous of all Indian chicken dishes is traditionally cooked in a clay oven, but admirably authentic results can be obtained using gas or electricity. The marinaded chicken pieces can also be grilled, barbecued or spit roasted.

1 fresh chicken, weighing approximately 3½ lb (1.5 kg)
1 medium onion, minced or finely chopped
3 cloves garlic, chopped
1 teaspoonful fresh ginger, chopped
1 cup natural unsweetened yoghurt
rind and juice of 1 lemon
2 tablespoonsful vinegar
1 teaspoonful paprika
2 teaspoonsful garam masala
2 teaspoonsful coriander powder

1 teaspoonful cumin powder
½ teaspoonful red food colouring
2 tablespoonsful ghee

Garnish
lettuce
onion rings
cucumber slices
lemon wedges

Remove the skin from the chicken and cut it into two. Using a
sharp knife make slanting incisions 1 in (2.5 cm) long in the
chicken on each limb and breast, taking care not to cut through to
the bone. In a large non-metallic bowl mix all the remaining
ingredients, except the ghee. Marinade the chicken in this spicy
yoghurt mixture for between 8 and 24 hours, turning occasionally
to ensure that all sides become uniformly soaked.

Heat the oven to Gas Mark 8/450°F. Place the chicken on a wire
rack or a baking tray. Cover with foil and roast on the top shelf for
1 hour. Baste the chicken with the marinade mixture once during
the cooking. Prior to serving, heat the ghee, pour over the chicken
halves and ignite. Serve the chicken on a bed of lettuce garnished
with onion rings, cucumber slices and lemon wedges. Serve with
chappatis.

Serves 2–3

Chicken Teriyaki

Japanese teriyaki dishes are in general best barbecued or cooked
directly over the flame.

1 × 3½ lb (1.5 kg) fresh chicken
2 cloves garlic, chopped
2 teaspoonsful fresh ginger, chopped
1 tablespoonful oil
½ teaspoonful brown sugar
4 tablespoonsful sake
½ cup soy sauce
a pinch of ajinomoto

Cut the chicken into joints. Mix the rest of the ingredients in a
large bowl and marinade the chicken joints for at least 2 hours.
Place the chicken on a wire rack and bake uncovered on the top

shelf of the oven at Gas Mark 5/375°F for about 20 minutes per side, basting with the marinade at least twice during cooking. The marinaded chicken could also be barbecued.

Serves 4

Singgang Ayam (Indonesian Spiced Grilled Chicken)

4 oz (113 g) creamed coconut
1½ cups boiling water
4 red chillies, de-seeded
3 cloves garlic, chopped
1 teaspoonful fresh ginger, grated
8 black peppercorns
⅛ teaspoonful turmeric
1½ teaspoonsful salt
1 medium onion, chopped
1 × 3 lb (1.3 kg) chicken
1 stalk lemon grass or ½ teaspoonful grated lemon rind
2 lemon or lime leaves, if available

Dissolve the creamed coconut in the boiling water. Using a pestle and mortar or an electric blender, grind the chillies, garlic, ginger, peppercorns, turmeric, salt and onion to a smooth paste. Cut the chicken lengthwise into two, along the breast bone. Wash and pat dry. Rub the ground ingredients on the chicken and leave for half an hour. In a shallow wide pan bring the coconut milk, the lemon grass and citrus leaves to the boil. Add the chicken to it and allow to simmer over a low heat until the chicken is cooked and the liquid evaporated. Just prior to serving grill the chicken on a barbecue or cooker, basting frequently with the spices.

Serves 4

Ayam Panggang

Grilled chicken Indonesian style.

1 × 3 lb (1.3 kg) chicken
1 medium onion, chopped
4 red chillies (optional)
4 cloves garlic, chopped

$\frac{1}{2}$ teaspoonful dried shrimp paste (trasi)
4 oz (113 g) creamed coconut
1$\frac{1}{4}$ cups boiling water
$\frac{1}{2}$ oz (14 g) tamarind
1 stalk lemon grass or $\frac{1}{2}$ teaspoonful grated lemon rind
1$\frac{1}{2}$ teaspoonsful brown sugar
1$\frac{1}{2}$ teaspoonsful salt

Cut the chicken lengthwise into two along the breast bone. Wash and pat dry with kitchen paper. Grind the onion, the chillies, the garlic and the trasi to a fine paste. Rub the chicken with the ground ingredients and leave covered for half an hour. Dissolve the creamed coconut in one cup of the boiling water, soaking the tamarind in the rest. Mash the tamarind with a fork, strain through a fine sieve, discard the pulp and reserve the liquid. Place the chicken in a wide shallow pan. Pour over the coconut milk and the tamarind water. Add the rest of the ingredients and bring to the boil. Simmer uncovered until the chicken is cooked; the chicken halves should remain whole although cooked through.

Ideally the chicken should now be grilled on charcoal until the skin is brown and crisp. Alternatively it can be roasted on a rack in a hot oven for about half an hour. During this final stage of cooking the chicken can be basted with the liquid in which it was boiled.

Serves 4

Japanese Fried Chicken

Japanese butchers often sell de-boned and cubed chicken meat. If you feel energetic enough you could prepare the chicken breasts in this way for this recipe.

2 tablespoonsful soy sauce
1 teaspoonful fresh ginger, finely chopped
2 tablespoonsful mirin
4 chicken breasts
1 tablespoonful cornflour
oil for deep frying

In a bowl mix the soy sauce, the ginger and the mirin. Marinade the chicken breasts for about an hour. Dry the chicken on kitchen paper. Dust in the cornflour and deep fry until golden brown.

Serves 4

Spicy Fried Chicken

This Indian fried chicken is spicy and delicious and makes a welcome change from ordinary fried chicken.

1 teaspoonful garlic, crushed
½ teaspoonful chilli powder (optional)
1 teaspoonful green ginger, crushed
salt to taste
6 chicken drumsticks
5 fl oz (142 ml) natural unsweetened yoghurt
2 eggs, separated
1 teaspoonful flour
1 teaspoonful mint leaves, crushed
2 teaspoonsful coriander powder
6 fl oz (170 ml) vegetable oil

Make a paste of the garlic, chilli powder, ginger and salt and rub into the chicken. Pour the yoghurt over the chicken and place in a large pan. Cook over a low heat, simmering for about 15 minutes until all the liquid has evaporated. Make a batter of the egg yolks, flour, mint and coriander and rub over the pieces of chicken. Let the chicken dry out in a shallow tray for a couple of hours.

Whisk the egg whites. Heat the oil in a frying pan. Dip the marinaded chicken in egg white and fry until golden brown.

Serves 3

Kai Tord (Spicy Fried Chicken)

A Thai variant of Kentucky fried chicken!

2 chicken breasts
1 small coriander root, when available
3 cloves garlic
½ teaspoonful ground black pepper
½ teaspoonful salt
lard or peanut oil for deep frying

Remove the flesh from the chicken breasts. Pound the coriander root, garlic, pepper and salt to a smooth paste. Rub the chicken with the ground ingredients and marinade for 1 hour. Heat the oil and deep fry the pieces of chicken on a medium to high heat. Drain on kitchen paper and serve hot.

Serves 2

Toriniku Tatsuate-Age (Marinated Deep Fried Chicken)

This Japanese fried chicken should be crisp on the outside and has a subtle flavour of soy sauce and mirin. Popular with children!

1½ lb (680 g) boneless chicken flesh
2 tablespoonful soy sauce
2 tablespoonful mirin
½ teaspoonful salt
8 tablespoonful cornflour
oil for deep frying

Cut the chicken into bite-sized pieces. Mix the soy sauce, mirin and salt in a bowl and marinade the chicken pieces in it for about 2 hours. Pat the chicken pieces dry with absorbent paper, roll them in cornflour and deep fry a few pieces at a time until golden brown. Care should be taken to ensure that the oil is not smoking hot as this will result in an unpleasant flavour.

Serve on a platter attractively arranged with finely shredded lettuce.

Serves 4

Goma Yaki

This Japanese dish is quick and easy to prepare and the sesame seed garnish provides a crunchy texture with a distinctive flavour. It requires the flesh only from the chicken breast. Where boneless chicken breasts are not available, buy two medium sized fresh chickens and cut the white flesh away from the breast bone to give four large fillets.

2 large chicken breasts
3 teaspoonful soy sauce
1½ teaspoonful salt
3 tablespoonful sake
2 teaspoonful white sesame seeds
3 tablespoonful oil
lettuce for garnishing

Remove the skin and cut the flesh away from the breast bone so that you have four pieces of chicken. Using a sharp knife make small slanting incisions into each piece, taking care not to cut right through. Marinade the chicken for half an hour in the soy sauce,

the salt and the sake. In a heavy bottomed frying pan dry roast the
sesame seeds over a medium heat until they begin to sputter.
Remove from the pan and allow to get cold. Heat the oil in a frying
pan. Add the chicken and fry over a medium heat for about 4
minutes on each side until evenly browned. Sprinkle with the
roasted sesame seeds and serve on a bed of lettuce.

Serves 4

Yin-ya-chi-ssu

Chinese stir fried chicken with fresh bean sprouts is an inexpensive
delicacy that is easy to make and nutritious.

2 whole chicken breasts, about 12 oz (340 g) each
2 teaspoonsful cornflour
1 egg white, lightly beaten
1 teaspoonful salt
2 teaspoonsful Chinese rice wine or pale dry sherry
4 tablespoonsful vegetable oil
4 oz (113 g) fresh bean sprouts, rinsed in cold water

Using a very sharp knife de-bone the chicken breasts and cut the
meat into shreds approximately $\frac{1}{8}$ in (3mm) wide and 2 in (5 cm)
long. Place the chicken shreds in a large bowl and sprinkle the
cornflour over to coat lightly. Add the egg white, half a teaspoonful
of the salt, the wine, and mix thoroughly with a large wooden or
plastic spoon. In a wok or large frying pan heat three teaspoonsful
of the oil almost to smoking point. Add the bean sprouts and the
remaining salt and stir fry for a couple of minutes. Remove the
bean sprouts to a bowl and set aside. Pour the remainder of the oil
into the pan, heat for a couple of seconds and add the chicken
mixture. Stir fry over a high heat until the chicken turns white. Put
the bean sprouts back into the pan and stir fry, mixing in with the
chicken mixture for 1 minute. Pour into medium sized serving
dishes. Serve with rice or noodles.

Serves 4

Mizutaki

A versatile dish that is cooked at the table – which is typical of Japanese food. The word mizutaki literally means a pot of bubbling water in which a variety of ingredients can be cooked. The cooking process is so simple that it retains the natural flavour of the ingredients.

1 × 3 lb (1.3 kg) fresh chicken
1½ teaspoonsful salt
2 pints (1.2 l) water
a small piece of fresh ginger
1 medium onion, chopped
1 small Chinese cabbage
1 lb (454 g) bean curd
8 large mushrooms
1 can bamboo shoots
8 spring onions
½ cup soy sauce
juice of 1 large lemon
radish (daikon, if available)

Wash and cut the whole chicken into small pieces. In a large pan combine the chicken, salt, water, ginger and chopped onion. Bring to the boil. Cover and simmer for about an hour. Remove any scum and excess fat. Wash and cut the cabbage into 2 in (5 cm) pieces. Cut the bean curd into four cubes. Wash and dry the mushrooms, discard the stalks and cut each mushroom into two. Drain the bamboo shoots and cut into slices. Wash the spring onions and cut into diagonal strips. Arrange the prepared ingredients on a large platter.

Make a sauce by mixing the soy sauce with the lemon juice. Pour a little sauce into individual bowls, one for each guest. Grate a small amount of radish and leave on the table.

Once the guests are seated bring the chicken stock to the boil and place the pan on a gas ring or fondue stove on the table. Add a selection of the vegetables to the simmering stock and cook for about 5 minutes or until they are done. Like sukiyaki, each guest helps himself to a selection of chicken and vegetables from the simmering pot which he dips into the sauce before eating. The sauce can be flavoured with the grated radish to suit individual taste. Serve a bowl of rice per guest.

Serves 4

Panthay Kaukswe

A popular Burmese dish which is not too spicy and is well suited to the Western palate.

1 × 3½–4 lb (1.5–1.8 kg) fresh chicken
3 large onions
6 cloves garlic
5 teaspoonsful fresh ginger, chopped
2 teaspoonsful dried shrimp paste
4 tablespoonsful sesame oil or vegetable oil
1 teaspoonful turmeric
2 teaspoonsful chilli powder (optional)
2 teaspoonsful salt
3 cups hot water
7 oz (198 g) creamed coconut
3 tablespoonsful chick pea flour

Cut the chicken into convenient sized pieces. Chop the onions and garlic. Using either an electric blender or a pestle and mortar, grind the onions, garlic, ginger and the shrimp paste to a smooth purée. In a heavy bottomed pan heat the oil and fry the ground ingredients over a medium to low heat for about 6 minutes. Add the chicken pieces and continue to fry for a further 5 minutes. Add the turmeric, chilli and salt. Add the hot water and bring rapidly to the boil. Cover and simmer for 45 minutes or until the chicken is cooked. Dissolve the creamed coconut over a low heat in half a cup of water and add it to the chicken. Mix the chick pea flour to a smooth paste with a little cold water, add it to the chicken and continue to cook for a further 10 minutes.

Serve the curry in a large bowl with extra fine egg noodles or cellophane noodles. The guests help themselves to noodles, ladle over the chicken and the gravy and add various accompaniments, which are served in separate bowls.

Accompaniments
finely sliced spring onions
lemon wedges
roasted chick pea flour
sliced garlic, deep fried to a pale brown colour
whole dried chillies, deep fried
fresh coriander leaves, finely chopped

Serves 4

Chetha Se Biyan

A Burmese speciality, this mild dry chicken dish is relished by those who do *not* like very spicy food.

2 large onions
4 cloves garlic
2 teaspoonsful fresh ginger, finely chopped
2 stalks lemon grass or 1 teaspoonful lemon rind, finely chopped
4 tablespoonsful vegetable oil
1 ×4 lb (1.8 kg) fresh chicken, cut into small pieces
1½ teaspoonsful turmeric
1 teaspoonful chilli powder
2 teaspoonsful salt
2 tablespoonsful coriander leaves, chopped

Finely chop the onions and garlic. Using either an electric blender or a pestle and mortar, grind the onions, garlic, ginger and lemon grass to a smooth paste. In a heavy bottomed pan heat the oil until it is smoking hot. Add the ground ingredients and stir fry for about 10 minutes over a medium to low heat. When the moisture has evaporated and the oil separates from the ground ingredients and floats on the surface, add the chicken pieces and mix thoroughly. Add the turmeric, chilli powder and salt and bring to the boil. Cover and simmer for about 50 minutes or until the chicken is cooked. Take care to stir the chicken occasionally to prevent it from sticking to the bottom of the pan. Prior to serving add the chopped coriander leaves.

Serves 4–6

Sate Ajam

A chicken sate from Indonesia. Ideally the meat should be grilled on charcoal but an electric grill is a suitable substitute.

4 chicken breasts
4 tablespoonsful soy sauce
3 tablespoonsful peanut oil
1½ teaspoonsful salt
1 teaspoonful ground black pepper
peanut sauce (Sans Katjang) – half quantity (see BASIC RECIPES)

Remove the chicken flesh from the bone and cut into bite-sized cubes. In a shallow dish mix the soy sauce, peanut oil, salt and pepper. Thread the meat on metal skewers, about four cubes per skewer. Arrange the skewers in the marinade mixture and leave for half an hour, turning the skewers over once during that time. Grill the meat on a high heat, turning the skewers over until all sides are evenly browned. Baste frequently with the marinade mixture during the cooking. Arrange the skewers on a shallow dish and pour over the peanut sauce before serving.

Serves 4

Kai Panen (Chicken in Coconut)

Coconut grows in great abundance in Thailand and is used liberally in much of the cooking there. Here the flavour of creamed coconut blends subtly with the chicken and other ingredients.

3 oz (84 g) creamed coconut
2 cups hot water
1 × 3–4 lb (1.3–1.8 kg) chicken
6 peppercorns
1½ teaspoonsful caraway seeds
1½ teaspoonsful coriander seeds
2 red chillies
5 cloves garlic
1 tablespoonful roasted peanuts
2 teaspoonsful dried lemon grass or grated lemon rind
1 tablespoonful fish sauce (nam pla)
½ teaspoonful salt
1 coriander root, when available
1 teaspoonful sugar
1 teaspoonful kapi
coriander leaves

Over a low heat dissolve the creamed coconut in the hot water. Wash the chicken and place it in a large saucepan. Pour the creamed coconut over it and bring to the boil. Cover and simmer for about 1 hour or until the chicken is cooked. Remove the chicken to a serving bowl and keep warm. Boil the liquid in which the chicken was cooked until it is reduced to about a cupful. Using a pestle and mortar or an electric blender grind the peppercorns, caraway seeds and coriander. Add the chillies and the garlic and the rest of the ingredients and blend to a smooth paste. Add the spices to the boiling liquid and cook for 5 minutes. Pour over the chicken and garnish with coriander leaves, when available.

Serves 4

Tsukune (Minced Chicken Rissoles)

This Japanese dish could be served either as a starter or as a main
course.

1 lb (454 g) chicken flesh
1 tablespoonful soy sauce
½ teaspoonful salt
1 teaspoonful sugar
1 tablespoonful mirin
1 egg yolk
4 tablespoonsful oil
1½ tablespoonsful sake
1 tablespoonful soy sauce
3 tablespoonsful water

Finely mince the chicken. Add 1 tablespoonful soy sauce, salt,
sugar, mirin and the egg yolk. Mix thoroughly. Divide into twenty-
five and mould into regular round shapes to resemble small
hamburgers. Heat the oil in a frying pan and fry the chicken
rissoles a few at a time until browned on both sides. Combine the
sake, soy sauce and water in a wide pan and bring to a boil. Add
the browned rissoles and boil for about 10 minutes or until all the
sauce has evaporated.

Serves 5

Yakitori (Kebabs, Japanese-style)

These chicken kebabs are delicious barbecued on charcoal, but they
can also be grilled on an electric or gas cooker.

12 oz (340 g) white chicken flesh, de-boned
4 oz (113 g) chicken livers
2 kidneys (lamb or pig)
2 green peppers
1 large onion
4 tablespoonsful sake
4 tablespoonsful soy sauce
1 tablespoonful sugar
½ tablespoonful fresh ginger, grated
a pinch of MSG

Cut the chicken, the livers and kidneys into bite-sized pieces.
Remove the seeds and cut the peppers and onion into bite-sized

pieces. Lightly grease eight metal skewers. Thread the meat and vegetables onto the skewers. In a pan bring the sake, soy sauce, sugar, ginger and MSG to the boil. Arrange the skewers on a shallow dish and pour over the hot marinade. Let stand for 15 minutes. Turn the skewers over and allow to stand in the marinade for a further 15 minutes. Heat the grill and cook the kebabs for about 5 minutes on each side or until the meat is cooked. Baste the kebabs with the marinade mixture a few times during the cooking.

Serves 4

Tsui-chi (Drunk Chicken!)

Drunk chicken is a Chinese speciality that can be served either as an hors d'oeuvre or a main course.

1 chicken weighing about 4 lb (1.8 kg)
3 pints (1.7 l) chicken stock
1 teaspoonful fresh ginger, chopped
1 spring onion, cut into 2 in (5 cm) lengths
½ pint (284 ml) Chinese rice wine or pale dry sherry
4 teaspoonsful salt

Place the chicken in a large heavy bottomed pan and cover with the chicken stock. Add the ginger and onion and bring to a rapid boil. Cover the pan, lower the heat and simmer for 20 minutes. Now turn off the heat and let the chicken cool in the pan (lid on) for about 3 hours. Pour ½ pint (284 ml) of the stock into a large bowl, combine with the wine and set aside. Next, using a sharp knife, cut the chicken into quarters, two breast pieces and two leg pieces, discarding the backbone. Cut each of these into two again. Sprinkle and rub two teaspoonsful of the salt over the chicken. Arrange the chicken pieces in a shallow baking dish. Pour the wine and stock mixture over the chicken, cover the dish with cling film or foil and refrigerate for two days, turning the pieces over occasionally. To serve, drain the chicken of all the liquid and chop the chicken (bones included) into chunks approximately 2×1 in (5×2.5 cm). Arrange on a platter with a salad.

Serves 4

Peking Duck

A famous Chinese dish that can be made with readily available ingredients. Ideal as one course at a special Chinese banquet!

$1 \times 4\frac{1}{2}$ lb (2 kg) duck
$2\frac{1}{2}$ cups water
3 tablespoonsful honey
2 teaspoonsful salt
5 slices fresh ginger
3 spring onions cut into 1 in (2.5 cm) lengths

To serve
mandarin pancakes (see SWEETS)
spring onions
hoi sin sauce

Wash the duck under running cold water and pat dry with kitchen towel. Tie a piece of string about 18 in (45 cm) round the neck of the duck and hang it in a cool airy place for about 3 hours. In a small pan combine the water, honey, salt, ginger and spring onions. Bring the pan to the boil and remove from the heat. Rub the surface of the duck with this mixture, making sure that every bit of the duck is well coated with the liquid. Discard the liquid and hang the duck again in a cool airy place for 2 hours. Preheat the oven to Gas Mark 5/375°F. Half fill a roasting tin with hot water and place a rack on top of it. Place the duck on the rack and roast for 1 hour. Reduce the heat to Gas Mark 2/300°F, turn the duck over and roast for a further 45 minutes. Now increase the heat to Gas Mark 5/375°F and continue to roast until the skin is crisp and evenly browned. Serve with mandarin pancakes, spring onion 'brushes' and hoi sin sauce.

To make spring onion brushes, wash the spring onions, trim off the roots and cut into 3 in (7.5 cm) lengths. At each end make four or five axially intersecting slits of about 1 in (2.5 cm). Immerse in iced water and refrigerate until the ends curl. Allow about 4 onion brushes per person.

To serve Peking Duck, remove the skin and cut into small pieces. Finely slice the meat with a sharp knife. Serve on a heated platter. Each guest places a piece of skin on the pancake, dips a spring onion brush into the hoi sin sauce, brushes it over the pancake and places a piece of meat on the pancake. He or she then rolls up the pancake and eats it.

Serves 4–6

Szechwan Duck

The duck in this recipe should be steamed and then deep fried whole in a wok. It is simpler to roast the duck on a wire rack over a pan of hot water. The result is equally good and much less trouble.

1 × 4½ lb (2 kg) duck
3 teaspoonsful whole peppercorns
3 teaspoonsful salt
2 teaspoonsful fresh ginger, finely grated
3 spring onions, finely chopped
1 tablespoonful soy sauce
1 teaspoonful five spice powder (available in Chinese grocery stores)
1 tablespoonful vegetable oil, preferably sesame

Wash the duck under running cold water and pat dry with kitchen towel. In a small heavy bottomed pan over a medium heat, dry roast the peppercorns for a few minutes, shaking the pan constantly so that they roast evenly. Coarsely crush the peppercorns in a mortar and pestle. In a bowl combine all the ingredients together and rub over the duck, including the cavity. Cover the duck in tin foil and place in the refrigerator for approximately 6 hours. Preheat the oven to Gas Mark 4/350°F. Half fill a roasting tin with hot water and place a rack on top of it. Place the duck on the rack and roast for 1½ hours. Uncover the duck and roast for a further 30 minutes, or until the duck is golden brown. Carve the duck and serve with mandarin pancakes or rice.

Serves 4–6

6

Meat Dishes

Kebabs

Traditionally cooked over live coals, kebabs reflect a Middle Eastern influence in north Indian cooking.

1 lb (454 g) mince
½ medium onion, ground or chopped finely
2 cloves garlic, chopped
½ teaspoonful fresh ginger
1 teaspoonful coriander
15 mint leaves, finely chopped
¼ teaspoonful powdered cinnamon
¼ teaspoonful powdered cloves
¼ teaspoonful powdered cardamom
1 teaspoonful salt
½ teaspoonful tomato purée
¼ teaspoonful freshly milled black pepper

In a bowl mix all the ingredients thoroughly. Divide into twelve portions. Shape into flat discs and grill until browned on both sides.

Serves 4

Luk Nua (Fried Meat Balls)

This is a delicious kofta-style meat ball preparation from Thailand.

8 oz (226 g) minced pork
8 oz (226 g) minced beef
4 cloves garlic, finely chopped
½ teaspoonful grated nutmeg
½ teaspoonful black pepper, ground
1 egg
1 teaspoonful salt
2 teaspoonsful fish sauce (nam pla)
1 tablespoonful spring onion, chopped
1 tablespoonful coriander leaves, finely chopped
oil for deep frying

Mix all the ingredients thoroughly in a bowl. Shape into walnut-sized balls. Deep fry a few at a time for about 4 minutes. Drain on kitchen paper.

Makes about 24, serves 4

Ame Hnat (Braised Beef)

This Burmese speciality could be served as an accompaniment to a rice or noodle dish.

1 lb (454 g) stewing beef
2 medium onions
4 cloves garlic
1 teaspoonful fresh ginger, finely chopped
4 tablespoonsful sesame oil or vegetable oil
¾ teaspoonful turmeric
1 teaspoonful chilli powder
¼ teaspoonful ground black pepper
1 teaspoonful salt
1 stalk lemon grass or ½ teaspoonful grated lemon rind
1¼ cups hot water
1 large onion
oil for deep frying

Cut the beef into 1½ in (3.5 cm) cubes. Grind the onions, garlic and ginger to a fine purée in an electric blender. In a medium sized saucepan heat the oil until smoking hot. Add the onion purée and stir fry for about 10 minutes over a medium to low heat. When the oil separates from the ground ingredients and floats on the surface add the beef. Fry the beef in this onion mixture for about 5 minutes. Add the rest of the ingredients and bring rapidly to the boil. Cover and simmer for about 1 hour or until the meat is tender. Remove the lid and continue to cook the beef over a medium heat until the liquid has evaporated and the meat is thickly coated with the gravy.

Finely slice the large onion and deep fry until golden brown. Garnish the meat with the fried onions just before serving.

Serves 4

Harak Mas Curry (Sri Lankan Beef Curry)

This Sri Lankan curry combines beef, spices and coconut.

2 tablespoonsful oil
1 medium onion, finely sliced
1 lb (454 g) braising beef, cut into 1 in (2.5 cm) pieces
3 cloves garlic
1 teaspoonful fresh ginger, finely chopped

$\frac{1}{4}$ teaspoonful turmeric
2 teaspoonsful malt vinegar
$\frac{1}{4}$ teaspoonful freshly milled black pepper
1 teaspoonful salt
1$\frac{1}{2}$ teaspoonsful coriander powder
1$\frac{1}{2}$ teaspoonsful cumin powder
3 cardamoms $\left.\right\}$ ground together
3 cloves
1 in (2.5 cm) stick cinnamon, ground
2 oz (56 g) creamed coconut
4 fl oz (113 ml) water
1 teaspoonful chilli powder
$\frac{1}{4}$ teaspoonful fenugreek

Heat the oil. Fry the onions. Add the meat and fry over a low heat until quite brown. Add the spices and other ingredients and simmer for 1 hour.

Serves 3

Pra Ram Lon Son (Rama-a-bathing)

A Thai delicacy made from good quality steak.

4 oz (113 g) creamed coconut
1$\frac{1}{4}$ cups hot water
4 cloves garlic
1 teaspoonful fresh ginger, finely chopped
$\frac{1}{2}$ medium onion, chopped
5 dried chillies (optional)
1 stalk lemon grass or 1 teaspoonful grated lemon rind
1 lb (454 g) fillet steak, finely sliced
2 teaspoonsful fish sauce (nam pla)
1 tablespoonful palm sugar
4 tablespoonsful peanut butter
8 oz (226 g) fresh or frozen spinach

Dissolve the creamed coconut over a medium heat in 1$\frac{1}{4}$ cups of hot water. Reserve two tablespoonsful of the coconut milk in a cup. Using a pestle and mortar or electric blender, mince the garlic, ginger, onion, chillies and lemon grass to a smooth paste. Bring the creamed coconut to the boil (except the two tablespoonsful) and add the finely sliced beef to it. Add the nam pla and sugar and allow to simmer for about 5 minutes. Remove the slices of beef from the coconut milk. Now add the blended ingredients to the coconut milk and allow to boil for a further 5 minutes. Add the peanut butter and mix thoroughly. In another pan boil 2 pints (1.2 l) of water. Add a teaspoonful of salt and the fresh spinach. Simmer for about 3 minutes and strain. (If frozen spinach is being used, follow the cooking instructions on the packet.) Arrange the spinach on a large serving platter, put the beef on top of it and pour the peanut sauce over. Lastly pour over the two tablespoonsful of coconut milk.

Serves 4

Kaeng Massaman (Muslim Curry)

A Thai dish in which whole spices are lightly roasted separately in a dry pan before being ground to a smooth paste together with kapi, onions, garlic and lemon grass. The roasted spices bring out an unusual aroma and make the curry look dark brown.

8 dried red chillies
2 tablespoonsful coriander seeds
1 tablespoonful caraway seeds
1 teaspoonful lemon grass or grated lemon rind
5 cloves
seeds of 5 cardamom pods
1 stick cinnamon
1 blade mace
$\frac{1}{4}$ teaspoonful grated nutmeg
8 bay leaves
5 cloves garlic
1 medium onion, chopped
$\frac{1}{2}$ teaspoonful kapi

In a heavy bottomed small pan, over a low to medium heat, lightly roast the spices separately until browned. Using a pestle and mortar grind all the ingredients to a smooth paste.

To make the curry you need
$\frac{1}{2}$ oz (14 g) tamarind
$2\frac{1}{4}$ cups boiling water
5 oz (140 g) creamed coconut
2 lb (900 g) stewing beef, cut into 1 in (2.5 cm) cubes
1 tablespoonful fish sauce (nam pla)
1 piece of cinnamon 2 in (5 cm) long

$\frac{1}{2}$ cup peanuts
2 teaspoonsful sugar
1 teaspoonful salt

Soak the tamarind in a quarter cup of the boiling water for 15 minutes. Bring the tamarind and water to the boil, simmer for about 3 minutes, mash with a fork and strain the tamarind through a sieve. Reserve the tamarind water and discard the pulp. Dissolve the creamed coconut in the rest of the boiling water. Add the meat, fish sauce, cinnamon and peanuts to the simmering coconut milk and boil over a low heat for about 1$\frac{1}{2}$ hours or until the meat is tender. Add the curry paste, sugar, salt and tamarind liquid and continue to simmer until the gravy is thick.

Serves 4–6

Empal Jawa

A Japanese steak dish.

1 lb (454 g) sirloin steak
$\frac{1}{2}$ oz (14 g) tamarind
$\frac{1}{4}$ cup boiling water
2 tablespoonsful peanut oil
1 large onion, chopped
3 cloves garlic, chopped
4 red chillies, finely chopped
$\frac{1}{2}$ teaspoonful dried shrimp paste (trasi)
1 teaspoonful salt
2 teaspoonsful brown sugar
1 stalk lemon grass or $\frac{1}{2}$ teaspoonful grated lemon rind
a few curry leaves, when available
2 tablespoonsful soy sauce

Place the meat in a pan, cover with cold water and bring to the boil. Simmer for 1 hour. Remove the meat from the stock and allow it to cool. Cut the meat into thin slices. Soak the tamarind in the boiling water, mash with a fork and strain the tamarind through a fine sieve. Discard the pulp and reserve the liquid. Heat the oil in a wok or large frying pan. Add the onions, garlic, red chillies, trasi and salt. Once the onions are softened and beginning to brown add the meat, sugar, lemon grass and curry leaves. Fry the meat over a low to medium heat for about 5 minutes. Finally add the soy sauce and continue to cook over a low heat until the meat becomes quite dry.

Serves 4

Rendang

An Indonesian steak dish.

1 teaspoonful coriander seeds
$\frac{1}{2}$ teaspoonful cumin
$\frac{1}{4}$ teaspoonful black peppercorns
$\frac{1}{4}$ teaspoonful fennel seeds
$\frac{1}{4}$ teaspoonful turmeric
1 large onion, chopped
1 teaspoonful fresh ginger, grated
3 cloves garlic, chopped
3 oz (85 g) creamed coconut
1 cup boiling water
$\frac{1}{2}$ oz (14 g) tamarind
1 stalk lemon grass or $\frac{1}{2}$ teaspoonful grated lime or lemon rind
a few curry leaves, when available
6 red chillies, finely chopped
1 teaspoonful salt
1 lb (454 g) rump steak, cut into 1 in (2.5 cm) cubes
1 teaspoonful brown sugar

In an electric blender grind the coriander, cumin, black peppercorns, fennel and turmeric. Add the onion, ginger and garlic and grind to a smooth paste. Dissolve the creamed coconut in three-quarters of a cup of boiling water. Dissolve the tamarind in a quarter cup of boiling water. Mash with a fork, strain, discard the pulp and reserve the tamarind liquid. Put all the ingredients except the sugar into a pan and bring to the boil. Simmer until almost all the liquid has evaporated. Add the sugar and continue cooking the meat over a low to medium heat until the meat is dry and the spices are nicely browned. In the last stage of cooking it is necessary to stir the meat constantly to prevent it from burning and sticking to the pan.

Serves 4

Abon (Shredded Meat, Indonesian Style)

Boiled meat is shredded and fried together with spices for this Indonesian speciality. It will keep for about three weeks in an airtight container. It is eaten with plain boiled rice and is sometimes added to omelettes.

1 lb (454 g) topside
2 cloves garlic
2 dried red chillies
1 small onion
2 teaspoonsful coriander powder
1 teaspoonful cumin powder
$\frac{1}{4}$ teaspoonful laos powder
1 teaspoonful salt
$\frac{1}{4}$ teaspoonful black pepper, ground
1 dessertspoonful lemon juice
1 teaspoonful brown sugar
2 oz (56 g) creamed coconut
$\frac{1}{4}$ cup boiling water
2 tablespoonsful peanut oil
2 onions, finely sliced
oil for deep frying

Put the meat in a pan and cover with cold water. Bring to the boil and simmer for about 2 hours or until the meat is so tender that it disintegrates. Drain the meat until it is quite dry. Using a grater, shred the meat until it resembles a pile of fibres. Grind the garlic, chilli and onion to a smooth paste in a blender. Add this to the meat together with the coriander, cumin, laos powder, salt, black pepper, lemon juice and brown sugar. Mix thoroughly. Dissolve the creamed coconut in the boiling water. If the meat mixture feels too dry, add a little coconut milk to bind the ingredients together. In a wok or frying pan heat the oil and fry the meat mixture over a medium heat until it is dry. Drain on kitchen paper. Deep fry the two finely sliced onions until golden brown. Mix the onion with the meat, cool to room temperature and store in an airtight container.

Sate Bumbu (Spiced Sate)

This Indonesian spiced sate dish is delicious. The meat is first cooked in spices and coconut milk and then grilled on charcoal.

1 lb (454 g) topside
1 teaspoonful coriander seeds
3 dried red chillies
2 macademia nuts or 2 whole almonds
1 teaspoonful fresh ginger, grated
3 cloves garlic, chopped
1 small onion, chopped
½ teaspoonful turmeric
2 tablespoonsful peanut oil
2–3 curry leaves, when available
1 stalk lemon grass or ½ teaspoonful grated lemon rind
2 teaspoonsful brown sugar
3 oz (85 g) creamed coconut
¾ cup boiling water

Cut the meat into 1 in (2.5 cm) cubes. In a blender grind the
coriander, chillies and nuts. Add the ginger, garlic, onions and
turmeric and grind to a smooth paste. If the paste is stiff add a
tablespoonful of oil to enable the blades to turn easily. Heat the oil
in a shallow frying pan. Add the blended ingredients and stir fry for
3 minutes. Add the curry leaves, lemon grass and brown sugar and
the meat and stir over a medium heat. Add the creamed coconut
which has been dissolved in three-quarters of a cup of boiling
water. Bring to the boil and cook, uncovered, until the water in the
sauce evaporates. Once the meat has cooled thread it on skewers
and grill on a charcoal fire or electric grill until evenly browned on
all sides.

Serves 4

Shabu Shabu

The name of this Japanese dish is supposed to describe the soft
bubbling sound that emanates from the pot while the ingredients
are being cooked. It is rather like fondue in that each guest cooks
his portion of meat and vegetables at the table to suit his own
taste.

12 mushrooms
12 spring onions
1 lb (454 g) bean curd
4 oz (113 g) Chinese cabbage or tender spinach leaves
2 lb (900 g) fillet steak
1 sachet (0.3 oz/9 g) dashinomoto
5 cups water

Sauce

3 tablespoonsful white sesame seeds
¾ cup dashi
1½ tablespoonsful mild vinegar
½ cup soy sauce
1 teaspoonful fresh ginger, finely grated
1 teaspoonful red peppers, finely chopped (optional)

Begin by preparing the sauce. Dry roast the sesame seeds in a heavy bottomed frying pan over medium heat until they begin to splutter. Remove from the pan and grind in a pestle and mortar. Mix all the sauce ingredients together in a large non-metallic container.

Wash the vegetables. Discard the stalks from the mushrooms. Cut the spring onions into diagonal strips. Cut the bean curd into cubes. Remove the stems from the cabbage leaves. Cut the beef into paper-thin slices. Arrange all the ingredients on a large platter.

In a pan bring the dashinomoto and water to the boil. Place the bubbling stock on a gas ring or fondue stove on the table. Each guest cooks pieces of meat in the bubbling stock to suit his individual taste. In Japan wooden chopsticks are used, but fondue forks are just as effective. Once the meat is cooked it is dipped into an individual bowl of sauce before it is eaten. Since the beef is very finely sliced the cooking should only take a couple of minutes. The vegetables are added to the stock and once all the ingredients have been cooked and eaten the broth is drunk in bowls. Serve plain boiled rice in individual bowls.

Serves 6

Beef Teriyaki

This is a rather simple Japanese preparation, but one with a distinctive seasoning and flavour.

2 cloves garlic, crushed
4 tablespoonsful mirin
6 tablespoonsful soy sauce
½ teaspoonful fresh ginger, finely grated
1 teaspoonful sugar
6 slices of ¼ in (6 mm) thick fillet steak
2 tablespoonsful oil

In a shallow dish mix together the garlic, mirin, soy sauce, ginger and sugar. Marinade the beef in this mixture for about half an hour, remembering to turn the slices of beef over after about 15 minutes. In a heavy bottomed frying pan heat the oil. Add the steaks and fry for about 2 minutes on each side. Pour over the remaining marinade liquid and allow to fry on a high heat for about 3 minutes. (The marinaded slices of beef can also be grilled.) Serve with boiled rice.

Serves 6

Sukiyaki

Perhaps the most famous of all Japanese dishes, sukiyaki is a dish that is cooked at the table. It consists of paper-fine slices of the best fillet steak, a wide selection of vegetables, bean curd and noodles cooked in sake and soy sauce. Each guest breaks an egg into a bowl and mixes it lightly with chopsticks. He then picks up slices of meat and vegetables from the cooking pot with his chopsticks to dip into the beaten egg before eating. Although the thought of a raw egg may not appeal to some, I must emphasize that the egg gets slightly cooked by the heat of the ingredients dipped into it.

2 lb (900 g) fillet steak
10 spring onions
3 leeks
1 lb (454 g) button mushrooms
1½ lb (680 g) bean curd
4 oz (113 g) fine cellophane noodles (shirataki)
1 can bamboo shoots
1 small Chinese cabbage
a small piece of suet
a jug of water
soy sauce
sake
sugar
6 eggs

Cut the beef into paper-fine slices. Wash the spring onions and leeks and cut into diagonal strips. Wash and dry the mushrooms and discard the stalks. Cut the bean curd into fairly large cubes. Boil the noodles whole, according to the instructions on the packet and allow to drain. Drain the bamboo shoots and cut into slices. Wash the cabbage, discard any tough outer leaves and cut into 2 in

(5 cm) pieces. Arrange all the ingredients in separate sections on a large platter.

Heat a sukiyaki pan or heavy bottomed large wide frying pan. Melt a piece of suet in the pan and add a few slices of beef to it. When the beef has slightly browned turn over and then add about two tablespoonsful of soy sauce, a tablespoonful of sake, a teaspoonful of sugar and a quarter cup of water. When the beef and sauce are bubbling, add about a third of each of the other ingredients remembering to include the leafy green vegetables last, as they require the least amount of cooking. Allow to cook for about 5 minutes. Each guest helps himself from the pan into his own bowl. The hostess must keep adding a supply of the various ingredients to the pan as the guests consume them. Sukiyaki is served with an individual bowl of rice per guest.

Serves 6

Teppan Yaki

Another Japanese dish that is cooked at the table on an iron rectangular griddle. The combination of beef and prawns is interesting.

12 oz (340 g) fillet steak
1 clove garlic
2 tablespoonsful soy sauce
1 tablespoonful mirin
4 fresh prawns
2 green peppers
2 spring onions
8 oz (226 g) bean sprouts

Dipping sauce
½ cup soy sauce
1 teaspoonful sugar
1 teaspoonful fresh ginger, finely grated
1 tablespoonful mirin
2 spring onions, finely chopped

Cut the beef into thin slices. Crush the garlic and mix it in a shallow dish with the soy sauce and mirin. Marinade the beef for about half an hour in this mixture. While the meat is marinading prepare the rest of the ingredients. Remove the shells and heads of the prawns and de-vein them. Cut the green peppers into thin strips, discarding the seeds. Cut the spring onions diagonally into 1½ in (2.5 cm) pieces. Wash and drain the bean sprouts.

In a small saucepan over a low heat bring the sauce ingredients to a boil. Simmer until the sugar has dissolved. Pour the sauce into four saucers.

Heat a heavy bottomed frying pan until it is hot. Lightly grease it with vegetable oil. Quickly stir fry the steak for about 3 minutes. Remove onto a warm plate. Now add the prawns, green peppers and spring onions and stir fry until the prawns and green peppers are cooked. Sprinkle a few drops of soy sauce into the pan while cooking. Remove onto a warm plate. Lastly add the bean sprouts and cook quickly, taking care to stir the bean sprouts during the cooking. Serve the steak, prawns and vegetables on a plate; each guest dips pieces of meat etc. into the sauce before eating.

Serves 4

Kashmiri Lamb Curry

This is a popular recipe for lamb in Kashmir.

1½ tablespoonsful ghee or oil
1½ lb (680 g) leg of lamb, cubed
3 teaspoonsful coriander powder
10 peppercorns, ground
6 cloves, ground
8 cardamoms, ground
¼ teaspoonful cinnamon powder
1 teaspoonful fresh ginger, finely chopped
½ teaspoonful salt
½ cup water
1 oz (28 g) ground almonds
3 fl oz (85 ml) double cream
blanched almonds
pistachio nuts

Heat the oil until it is smoking hot. Add the cubes of meat and allow to brown. Add the spices, salt and water and bring to the boil. Cover and simmer for 45 minutes. Just prior to serving mix the ground almonds with the cream and add to the meat. Cook on a low heat until the gravy starts to boil. Garnish with blanched almonds and pistachio nuts.

Serves 4

Kashmiri Lamb with Dried Fruit

An exotic and unusual blend of flavours!

$2\frac{1}{4}$ lb (1 kg) leg of lamb or mutton
1 teaspoonful allspice
$\frac{1}{2}$ teaspoonful ground black pepper
$\frac{1}{2}$ teaspoonful coriander powder
$\frac{1}{2}$ teaspoonful cumin powder
$1\frac{1}{2}$ teaspoonsful salt
2 medium onions, finely sliced
2 teaspoonsful fresh ginger, finely chopped
2 cloves garlic, finely chopped
1 cup unsweetened natural yoghurt
2 oz (56 g) ghee or butter
$\frac{1}{2}$ cup raisins
1 cup dried apricots
2 tablespoonsful pistachio nuts

Trim the fat off the meat and cut into bite-sized pieces. In a bowl mix the spices, salt, onions, ginger and garlic with the yoghurt. Add the meat and marinade for at least 6 hours. Heat the ghee and fry the raisins, apricots and nuts for about 2 minutes. Remove from the pan. Reheat the ghee and add the meat and marinade and stir on a high flame for about 5 minutes. Cover and simmer for 1 hour. Prior to serving add the dried fruit and nuts and reheat.

Serves 4

Korma Kambing

Many influences can be seen to merge together in Indonesian cooking.

1 tablespoonful coriander seeds
2 teaspoonsful cumin seeds
1 teaspoonful fennel seeds
$1\frac{1}{2}$ teaspoonsful black peppercorns
2 cardamom pods, de-seeded
2 teaspoonsful fresh ginger, grated
2 lb (900 g) leg of lamb, cut into cubes
2 tablespoonsful ghee or vegetable oil
$\frac{1}{2}$ medium onion, chopped
2 pieces cinnamon stick
8 whole cloves
7 cloves garlic, chopped

1 stalk lemon grass or ½ teaspoonful grated lemon rind
6 oz (168 g) creamed coconut
2 cups boiling water
8 oz (226 g) potatoes
2½ teaspoonsful salt

Grind the coriander, cumin, fennel, peppercorns, cardamom and ginger in an electric blender. Mix the ground ingredients into the meat and leave for about half an hour. In a large pan heat the ghee or the oil and fry the onion until pale brown. Add the cinnamon and cloves and continue to fry for a couple of minutes. Add the garlic, lemon grass and meat and allow to fry until the meat has lost its redness. Dissolve the creamed coconut in the boiling water and add to the meat. Bring to the boil and simmer, covered, for about 45 minutes. Peel and dice the potatoes into 1 in (2.5 cm) cubes. Add these and the salt to the meat and continue cooking for a further half hour or until the potatoes are cooked.

Serves 6–8

Gule Kambing

An Indonesian mutton curry.

3 tablespoonsful peanut oil
2 medium onions, chopped
1 in (2.5 cm) piece of cinnamon stick
4 cloves
3 cardamom pods
4 cloves garlic
2 teaspoonsful fresh ginger, grated
½ teaspoonful black peppercorns
6 dried chillies
½ teaspoonful nutmeg
3 macademia nuts or almonds
2 teaspoonsful ground coriander
½ teaspoonful turmeric
1 teaspoonful ground cumin
½ teaspoonful ground fennel
3 oz (85 g) desiccated coconut
½ oz (14 g) tamarind
1½ lb (680 g) leg of mutton or lamb, cut into cubes
1 stalk lemon grass or ½ teaspoonful grated lemon rind
1½ teaspoonsful salt
2 firm tomatoes, chopped
4 oz (113 g) creamed coconut

Heat the oil and fry the onions, cinnamon, cloves and cardamoms. In a blender grind the garlic, ginger, pepper, red chillies, nutmeg, macadamia nuts, coriander, turmeric, cumin and fennel. Add the ground ingredients to the onions and fry for about 3 minutes. In a heavy bottomed frying pan dry roast the desiccated coconut until pale brown. Soak the tamarind in a quarter cup of boiling water for 5 minutes, mash with a fork and strain through a fine sieve. Discard the pulp and reserve the liquid. Add the meat to the spices and fry until well mixed. Add the coconut, tamarind liquid, lemon grass, salt, tomatoes and the creamed coconut dissolved in two cups of boiling water. Bring the meat to the boil and simmer over the lowest possible heat for about 1½ hours.

Serves 6

Pork Spareribs

This is a Chinese favourite that combines easily with any meal.

2 lb (900 g) pork spareribs
4 tablespoonsful soy sauce
4 tablespoonsful golden syrup
3 cloves garlic, crushed
1 teaspoonful fresh ginger, crushed
1 tablespoonful vinegar
2 teaspoonsful salt
½ cup water

Combine all the ingredients in a medium sized pan. Bring to the boil and simmer until almost all the water has evaporated. Remove the meat from the pan and grill under a medium flame until evenly browned.

Serves 4

Barbecued Pork

A popular Chinese recipe.

1 lb (454 g) belly pork
1 teaspoonful fresh ginger, grated
2 cloves garlic, finely chopped

2 tablespoonsful hoi sin sauce
2 tablespoonsful soy sauce
1 tablespoonful Chinese rice wine or dry sherry
½ teaspoonful salt
½ teaspoonful five spice powder
2 tablespoonsful honey

Remove the pork rind and cut the meat into 1 in (2.5 cm) strips. In a shallow dish mix the ginger, garlic, hoi sin sauce, soy sauce, wine, salt and spices. Marinade the strips of pork in this for 1 hour. Place a greased rack over a roasting tin containing 1 in (2.5 cm) of hot water. Place the strips of pork on the rack. Glaze with the honey and bake for 45 minutes at Gas Mark 5/375°F.

Serves 2–3

Uru Mas Curry (Spicy Pork)

Pork curry, Sri Lankan style.

1½ lb (680 g) pork
8 oz (226 g) lambs' liver
2 fl oz (56 ml) vegetable oil
2 large onions, chopped
6 cloves garlic, chopped
1 teaspoonful chopped ginger
¼ teaspoonful freshly milled black pepper
1 teaspoonful cumin powder
½ teaspoonful turmeric
2 in (5 cm) stick cinnamon, ground
5 cloves, ground
1 teaspoonful salt
1 fl oz (28 ml) vinegar

Cut the pork and liver into bite-sized pieces, cover with a cup of water and cook for 30 minutes. In a large frying pan heat the oil and fry the pieces of pork and liver until brown. Remove the meat. Fry the onions and garlic in the remaining fat and add the spices and salt. Return the pork and liver to the pan and add the vinegar and half a cup of water. Simmer over a low heat until the meat is tender.

Serves 4–6

Sate Babi

An Indonesian delicacy.

1 lb (454 g) fillet of pork
1 small onion, finely chopped
2 cloves garlic, finely chopped
1 teaspoonful fresh ginger, grated
2 red chillies, chopped
1 tablespoonful lemon juice
2 tablespoonsful soy sauce
½ teaspoonful salt
1 tablespoonful peanut oil

Cut the meat into 1 in (2.5 cm) cubes. In a blender grind the onion, garlic, ginger and chillies. In a shallow dish mix all the ingredients except the pork. Thread the pork on skewers, about three pieces per skewer. Marinade the pork for about 1 hour, turning the pieces over once during that time. Cook the meat on a medium heat, turning the skewers over regularly and basting the meat frequently with the marinade liquid. The meat should be evenly browned on the outside and thoroughly cooked right through.

Serves 4

Ma Ho (Galloping Horses)

A subtle combination of flavours and textures makes this a superb Thai delicacy.

1½ tablespoonsful lard or oil
6 cloves garlic, crushed
8 oz (226 g) pork (lean and fat mixed), very finely minced
2 oz (56 g) roasted peanuts, finely chopped
2 tablespoonsful sugar
1 tablespoonful fish sauce (nam pla)
1 tablespoonful coriander leaves, chopped
mandarin oranges and pineapple slices, fresh or canned
1 fresh red chilli, finely sliced

Heat the lard or oil and lightly brown the garlic in it. Add the pork and stir fry for about 1 minute. Add the rest of the ingredients except the chilli and the fruit. Cook on a medium to low heat until the moisture has evaporated and the mixture is quite dry. Allow to cool. If using canned fruit, drain the fruit thoroughly. Cut the pineapple slices into bite-sized pieces. Spoon a little of the cooked mixture on top of each piece of pineapple and garnish with a piece of red chilli. Slit each orange segment so that it resembles a circular disc of orange. Spoon a little of the cooked mixture and garnish as for the pineapple.

Serves 6–8

Red Cooked Shoulder of Pork

A Chinese speciality. One of many pork dishes in the Chinese culinary repertoire.

$4\frac{1}{2}$ *lb (2 kg) shoulder of pork*
1 tablespoonful sugar
$\frac{1}{2}$ cup Chinese rice wine or dry sherry
$\frac{3}{4}$ cup soy sauce
1 cup cold water
1 whole star anise
1 slice fresh ginger

Place the pork in a heavy bottomed saucepan, just large enough to hold it. Add the rest of the ingredients and bring rapidly to the boil. Cover and simmer the pork for about 2–3 hours, turning the piece of meat over several times during the cooking. The meat should be tender and the liquid reduced to about a cup. Carefully remove the pieces of meat onto a serving dish. Pour the sauce over and serve hot.

Serves 6–8

Sweet and Sour Pork

A Chinese recipe.

1 lb (454 g) lean pork
3 oz (85 g) cornflour
2 oz (56 g) plain flour
1 teaspoonful salt
1 egg
3 tablespoonsful cold water
oil for deep frying

Sweet and sour sauce
1 green pepper
2 carrots
1 tablespoonful cornflour
1 tablespoonful water
2 cloves garlic
2 tablespoonsful sugar
1 tablespoonful soy sauce
3 tablespoonsful wine vinegar
1 tablespoonful Chinese rice wine or dry sherry
1 small onion, chopped
½ teaspoonful fresh ginger, grated

Trim off any fat and cut the pork into 1 in (2.5 cm) cubes. In a bowl mix the cornflour, plain flour and salt. Separate the egg yolk from the white. Lightly mix the egg yolk and the water. Make a well in the centre of the flour and work in the egg and water to form a smooth batter. Beat the egg white until stiff. Fold into the batter. Heat the oil until it is smoking hot. Drip a few pieces of pork into the batter and deep fry until golden brown and crisp. Drain on kitchen paper and keep warm in a low oven until all the pieces are fried.

To make the sauce, wash and cut the green pepper into convenient size squares. Peel the carrots and slice lengthwise into 1 in (2.5 cm) pieces. Mix the cornflour with the water. Finely chop the garlic. In a small bowl mix together the sugar, soy sauce, vinegar and wine. In a wok or frying pan heat a tablespoonful of oil until it is smoking hot. Add the onion, carrots and pepper and stir fry over a medium heat for 2 minutes. Add the ginger and garlic and the soy sauce, vinegar, wine and sugar. Allow to boil for 1 minute. Add the cornflour and cook for about half a minute until the sauce has thickened and becomes clear. Arrange the pork pieces on a serving dish and pour the sauce over. Serve at once.

Serves 4

Pork with Bean Curd

A Chinese speciality combining several distinctive flavours.

6 dried Chinese mushrooms
1 lb (454 g) fillet of pork
3 tablespoonsful soy sauce

1 tablespoonful Chinese rice wine or dry sherry
¾ teaspoonful salt
½ teaspoonful sugar
8 oz (226 g) bean curd
2 tablespoonsful oil
½ tablespoonful cornflour

Soak the mushrooms in hot water for 30 minutes. Discard the stems and finely slice the caps. Cut the pork into fine strips about 2 × 1 in (5 × 2.5 cm). In a bowl mix the soy sauce, wine, salt and sugar and marinade the pork in this for 30 minutes. Cut the bean curd into cubes. Heat the oil in a wok or frying pan. When the oil is smoking hot add the pieces of pork and stir fry for 3 minutes. Add the mushrooms and continue to cook for a further 2 minutes. Add the bean curd and the marinade liquid and bring rapidly to the boil. Mix the cornflour into a smooth paste with a little cold water, add it to the bubbling dish and stir until thickened. Serve at once.

Serves 4–6

Stir-fried Snow Peas and Meat

A Thai speciality combining the flavours of several different ingredients – snow peas, pork and shrimp.

1 lb (454 g) snow peas
4 oz (113 g) fillet of pork
4 oz (113 g) shrimp
1 oz (28 g) lard or vegetable oil
5 cloves garlic, finely chopped
3 teaspoonsful fish sauce (nam pla)
1 teaspoonful sugar
¼ teaspoonful freshly milled black pepper

Wash the peas and allow to drain. Cut the pork and shrimp into small pieces. Heat the oil or lard and brown the garlic in it. Add the pork and shrimp and stir fry over a medium heat for a couple of minutes until cooked. Add the peas and the rest of the ingredients and stir fry over a medium to high heat until the peas are cooked.

Serves 4–6

Sate Padang (Sate from Sumatra)

Padang food in general is rather hot to the average taste so be
wary in the use of chillies.

2 teaspoonsful coriander seeds
1 teaspoonful cumin seed
½ teaspoonful black peppercorns
8 dried red chillies
1 small onion, chopped
3 cloves garlic, chopped
1 teaspoonful fresh ginger, grated
¼ teaspoonful turmeric
1 lb (454 g) liver or heart
1 teaspoonful salt
1 stem lemon grass or ½ teaspoonful grated lemon rind
1 oz (28 g) ground rice

Grind the coriander, cumin, black peppercorns and chillies in an
electric blender. Add the onions, garlic, ginger and turmeric and
grind to a smooth paste. Cut the meat into even-sized cubes. Put
the meat into a pan with the salt and one cup of water, the lemon
grass and half the ground spices. Bring to the boil and simmer,
uncovered, for half an hour. Thread the meat on skewers and cook
over a low to medium heat, turning the skewers regularly until the
meat is evenly browned on all sides. Add the other half of the
spices to the liquid in which the meat was cooked and bring to the
boil. Mix the ground rice to a smooth paste with a little cold water.
Add it to the boiling sauce, stirring until the mixture has thickened.
Arrange the skewers on a shallow serving dish, pour the sauce over
and serve.

Serves 4

Ma Uon

A Thai dish with a blend of several subtle flavours, this savoury
steamed custard is delicious and can be made in advance. It is
excellent as a starter or for a snack meal.

½ cup chicken meat
½ cup pork
½ cup cooked crabmeat
1 oz (28 g) creamed coconut

2 tablespoonsful boiling water
1 tablespoonful garlic, finely chopped
2 tablespoonsful chopped coriander, including roots and stem
2 tablespoonsful fish sauce (nam pla)
2 teaspoonsful soft brown sugar
2 eggs
1 tablespoonful spring onions, finely sliced

Finely chop or mince the chicken and pork. Flake the crabmeat and chop it finely. Dissolve the creamed coconut in the boiling water and allow to cool. In a bowl mix together the chicken, pork and crabmeat. Add the garlic, coriander, fish sauce, creamed coconut and sugar. Break the eggs into a bowl and reserve one yolk for glazing. Beat the eggs until pale and foamy. Add to the meat mixture and stir thoroughly. Divide into twelve small bowls or cups. Lightly mix the remaining egg yolk and brush over the top. Sprinkle with the spring onions and steam for 20–30 minutes, until a knife, when inserted, comes out clean. Cool and remove from the cups.

Serves 3–4

7

Seafood Dishes

Ho Mok (Steamed Fish)

A speciality of Thailand. Traditionally this spicy fish is steamed in banana leaves. Since banana leaves are hard to come by in the West, you could use tin foil as a wrapping or cook the fish in a shallow heatproof dish.

1½ lb (680 g) filleted white fish
3 oz (85 g) creamed coconut
¾ cup hot water
3 dried red chillies
¾ teaspoonful turmeric
1 teaspoonful salt
4 cloves garlic, chopped
8 peppercorns
½ teaspoonful dried lemon grass or grated lemon rind
1 egg
2 tablespoonsful fish sauce (nam pla)
3 tablespoonsful coriander leaves, finely chopped
3 tablespoonsful spring onions, finely chopped

Remove the skin and bones from the fish and cut into slices. Over a low heat dissolve the creamed coconut in the hot water. Allow to cool. Using an electric blender blend together the chillies, turmeric, salt, garlic, peppercorns and lemon grass. In a large bowl mix the ground ingredients with the egg, the fish sauce and half the cooled coconut milk. Add the sliced fish and turn it over until it has absorbed most of the liquid. Cut four squares of tin foil, each about 1 ft (0.3 m) square. Place a piece of foil on a plate and put a quarter of the marinaded fish on it. Sprinkle with coriander leaves and spring onion and spoon one-fourth of the coconut milk over the fish. Fold the foil over the fish to make a neat parcel. Repeat the process until you have four neat parcels of fish. Place in a colander and steam for 30 minutes. Serve with boiled rice.

Serves 4

Tempura

With the possible exception of sukiyaki, tempura is perhaps the best known of Japanese dishes outside Japan. A selection of prawns, fish and vegetables is dipped in batter and deep fried at the table. It is a versatile dish in that any combination of vegetables and fish that is available can be used. The success of the dish is dependent on the batter, which should be made just prior to use, and the temperature of the oil, which should be about 175°C (350°F).

3 lb (1.3 kg) filleted white fish
8 prawns
1 lotus root (canned)
a handful of French beans
a few spinach leaves
1 onion
1 medium aubergine
1 green pepper
8 fresh mushrooms
3 cups vegetable oil
1 cup sesame oil

Batter
1 large egg
1½ cups ice-cold water
1 cup plain flour
⅓ cup cornflour

Wash the fish, remove the skin and slice into strips of about $2 \times 1\frac{1}{2}$ in (5×3.5 cm). Shell and de-vein the prawns leaving the tails on. Cut the lotus root into $\frac{1}{4}$ in (6 mm) slices. Wash and string the beans. Wash and dry the spinach leaves. Cut the onion and the aubergine into $\frac{1}{4}$ in (6 mm) slices. De-seed the green peppers and cut into strips. Wash the mushrooms, remove the stalks and leave whole. Take care that the ingredients are thoroughly dry (use kitchen paper). Arrange all the ingredients on a large platter and keep in a cool place until needed. To prevent discoloration the aubergines should be cut at the last minute.

Heat the oil over a medium flame. While the oil is heating beat together the eggs and ice-cold water. Sift the flour and put it all into the egg mixture. Lightly mix the flour with the liquid. Do not beat. It does not matter if the batter is slightly lumpy. Dip vegetables or fish into the batter a few pieces at a time and deep fry until very slightly browned. The frying should only take a couple of minutes, even less for the vegetables. Allow the oil to heat up to temperature again between successive additions of ingredients to be fried. Since the frying is done at the table, the dish is served literally from the frying pan.

Serves 4

Saba no Sutataki (Soused Mackerel)

This inexpensive Japanese fish dish is easy to make and it is delicious.

1 large mackerel weighing about 1 lb (454 g)
salt
¾ cup white wine vinegar
2 tablespoonsful sugar
½ cup soy sauce
1 teaspoonful sugar
¼ cup wine vinegar
2 teaspoonsful fresh ginger, grated
2 oz (56 g) carrots, cut into strips
2 oz (56 g) Japanese radish, cut into fine strips
watercress or parsley for garnish
2 tablespoonsful wasabi powder (mixed with a little cold water)

Wash and clean the fish and remove the head, skin and bones. Cut the fish into thin slices. Liberally coat the sliced fish with salt and allow to stand for 4 hours in a cool place. Mix the first lot of vinegar and sugar in a shallow dish. Pat the fish dry on paper and marinade in this mixture for half an hour. In a small pan bring the soy sauce, sugar, vinegar and grated ginger to a boil. Strain and allow to get cold.

Arrange the fish attractively on a plate together with the carrots and radish. Garnish with the watercress or parsley. Serve the sauce in individual small saucers. Each guest mixes a little wasabi into his or her portion of sauce and dips the fish into it before eating.

Serves 4

Yosenabe

This is a rather versatile 'all in one' Japanese dish that is cooked at the table. You can use any kind of meat or fish, and any vegetables that are to hand. If the fish stock (dashi) does not appeal to you, use chicken stock instead.

1 sachet (0.3 oz/9 g) dashinomoto
4 cups water
⅓ cup soy sauce
8 fresh mushrooms
4 oz (113 g) fresh spinach leaves

4 spring onions
4 oz (113 g) prawns
1 lb (454 g) any white fish, filleted
1 lb (454 g) bean curd
4 oz (113 g) kamaboku (fish sausage)
1 large carrot
8 oz (226 g) noodles, preferably udon, boiled

In a pan mix the dashinomoto with the water, then add the soy sauce. Wash and dry the mushrooms, discarding the stalks. Wash the spinach leaves and remove the stems. Wash the spring onions and cut into diagonal strips. Wash and de-vein the prawns. Wash the fish and cut into long, narrow pieces large enough for one mouthful. Cut the bean curd into cubes. Slice the fish sausage. Slice the carrot and boil it. Arrange all the prepared ingredients on a large platter. Bring the stock to the boil and, once the guests are seated, add a selection of ingredients to the bubbling pot. The guests help themselves from the pan into their own bowl. The hostess should keep adding a supply of ingredients to the pan as needed. Serve with a bowl of rice per guest.

Serves 4

Sashimi

This Japanese raw fish hors d'oeuvre is an unusual delicacy. If you can get very fresh fish it is easy to make and will be a great success; and it is preferable to buy the fish whole and prepare it at home. However, frozen sashimi is available in the West from Japanese grocery stores.

1 medium sized very fresh tuna, sea bream or sole
2 tablespoonsful fresh ginger, grated
2 tablespoonsful horseradish powder (wasabi)
grated radish (daikon, if available)
watercress and lemon wedges for garnish
soy sauce

Cut off the fish head and tail and remove the entrails. Remove the skin and the backbone. Cut the fish lengthwise into two. Finely slice the fillets into rectangular pieces about $\frac{1}{4}$ in (6 mm) thick. Arrange a few pieces on each plate. Mix the horseradish powder to a stiff paste with a little cold water. Add a little grated radish and a dab each of grated ginger and horseradish on each plate. Garnish with a lemon wedge, and a sprig of watercress. Serve a small bowl or saucer of soy sauce per person. Each diner mixes a little ginger and horseradish into the soy sauce and dips a piece of sashimi into it before eating.

Serves 6

Tai-No Shio-Yaki

Grilled sea bream – Japanese style. Any medium sized fish can be cooked in this manner; small trout are particularly delicious. The fish is best barbecued on charcoal, but it can also be grilled.

2 sea bream, each weighing about 8 oz (226 g)
salt
4 thin metal skewers
4 stems young ginger, when available, or lemon wedges

Wash the fish and remove the scales. Make a small incision below the stomach fins and remove the entrails. Coat the fish generously with salt and allow to stand for half an hour. Pat the fish dry with kitchen paper. Lightly grease the skewers and insert through the tail to below the eye of the fish. Heat the grill and just prior to cooking coat the fish liberally with salt. Cover the tail with a piece of foil to prevent it burning. Grill the fish on a medium to hot heat for about 5 minutes on each side or until the fish is cooked. Serve garnished with young ginger stems or lemon wedges.

Serves 4

Panggang Ikan

Grilled fish the Indonesian way!

1 whole fish or 1½ lb (680 g) fish steaks
3 oz (85 g) creamed coconut
½ oz (14 g) tamarind
½ medium onion, chopped
2 red chillies, chopped
1 teaspoonful fresh ginger, chopped
2 cloves garlic, chopped
1 teaspoonful salt

1 stalk lemon grass or $\frac{1}{2}$ teaspoonful grated lemon rind
1 teaspoonful brown sugar
lemon wedges for garnish

Wash and clean the fish, leaving the head and tail intact. If using fish steaks wash in cold water. Dissolve the creamed coconut in a cup of boiling water. Bring the tamarind to the boil in a quarter cup of water and mash with a fork. Remove from the heat and strain, discarding the pulp and reserving the tamarind water. In a blender grind the onion, chillies, ginger and garlic. In a non-metallic shallow container combine the ground ingredients with the salt, tamarind water and coconut milk. Marinade the fish in this liquid for about an hour. On a medium to high heat grill the fish, basting frequently with the marinade mixture. Bring the remaining marinade mixture to the boil together with the lemon grass and sugar. Simmer for 2 minutes. Serve the fish on a platter garnished with lemon wedges. Serve with rice and the boiled marinade liquid.

Serves 3–4

Kai Kwam (Stuffed Fried Eggs)

A Thai speciality: the combination of seafood and pork gives the eggs an unusual flavour.

9 large eggs
1 cup boiled prawns, finely minced
1 cup cooked crabmeat
2 tablespoonsful fish sauce
$\frac{1}{4}$ teaspoonful black pepper
salt to taste
1 tablespoonful coriander leaves, finely chopped
oil for deep frying

Batter
$\frac{3}{4}$ cup plain white flour
$\frac{3}{4}$ cup water
$\frac{1}{2}$ teaspoonful salt

Place the eggs in a large pan, cover with cold water and bring slowly to the boil. Simmer for 6 minutes. Remove the eggs from the pan and, when cold enough to handle, shell them. Cut each egg lengthwise into two. Mix the egg yolks with the rest of the ingredients. Divide the mixture into eighteen portions. Fill each half egg white to resemble an egg.

In a bowl mix the flour with the water. Beat to a smooth elastic paste. Add salt. Dip each egg in this batter and deep fry a few at a time over a medium heat until evenly browned.

Serves 6–8

Sakana Kara-age (Fried Fish)

This Japanese dish makes a nice crisp fish starter.

1 lb (454 g) sprats or small mackerel
salt
oil for deep frying
cornflour
½ cup dashi
3 tablespoonsful soy sauce
2 tablespoonsful mirin
1 teaspoonful fresh ginger, grated

Remove the heads and entrails and wash the fish thoroughly. Sprinkle generously with salt and leave for 20 minutes. Pat the fish dry with kitchen paper. Heat the oil until it is hot. Dust the fish a few at a time in cornflour and deep fry until crisp. Drain on kitchen paper. In a small pan bring the dashi, soy sauce, mirin and ginger to the boil. Remove from the heat and allow to get cold. Serve the fish hot with an individual helping of the dipping sauce.

Serves 6

Pla Cian (Fried Fish)

Fish in one form or other is an important item of Thai food. The number and variety of fish dishes in Thailand would seem hard to beat.

1 ×2 lb (900 g) whole bream or snapper
½ oz (14 g) tamarind
½ cup water
⅓ cup oil or lard
4 cloves garlic, coarsely chopped
3 tablespoonsful soy sauce
1 tablespoonful fresh ginger, grated
1 level tablespoonful palm sugar or light brown sugar

1 tablespoonful fish sauce (nam pla)
5 spring onions, cut into 1 in (2.5 cm) pieces
½ teaspoonful salt
coriander leaves for garnishing

Trim off the fins and clean the fish thoroughly, leaving the head and tail intact. Wash the fish and dry with a cloth or kitchen paper. Soak the tamarind in the water for 15 minutes. Put the tamarind and the water into a pan and bring to the boil. Simmer for 5 minutes. Strain the tamarind and reserve the liquid. In a large frying pan heat the lard or oil and fry the fish on both sides until lightly browned. Transfer the fish to a serving platter. In the same pan brown the garlic. Add the soy sauce, ginger, sugar, tamarind liquid, nam pla, spring onions and salt. Bring to the boil and simmer for about 3 minutes. Pour over the fish, garnish with coriander leaves and serve immediately.

Serves 2–3

Ikan Goreng

Fried fish, Indonesian style.

1 whole fish (bream, snapper or mackerel)
1 oz (28 g) tamarind
peanut oil for frying

Clean the fish and remove the scales leaving the head and tail intact. Make two slanting incisions on each side, taking care not to cut right through to the bone. Bring the tamarind to the boil in a cup of hot water. Mash the tamarind with a fork, remove from the heat and sieve, discarding the pulp and reserving the liquid. Once the tamarind water has cooled marinade the fish in it for half an hour. Pat the fish dry with kitchen towel and shallow fry on both sides until browned. Drain on kitchen paper and serve immediately.

Serves 2

Pla Prio Wan (Fried Fish with Ginger Sauce)

Yet another fish recipe from Thailand, exquisitely flavoured with a rich ginger sauce. The pickled red ginger can be obtained from oriental grocery stores.

1 ×2 lb (900 g) whole bream or snapper
seasoned flour
oil for frying
coriander leaves for garnishing

Trim off the fins and clean the fish thoroughly leaving the head and tail intact. Wash the fish and dry thoroughly with a cloth or kitchen paper. Using a sharp knife make two sets of evenly spaced slanting incisions almost to the bone, so as to form a diamond-shaped pattern on the fish. Rub the fish with oil and dust in seasoned flour before shallow frying in ½ in (1.3 cm) of hot oil. Turn the fish over carefully and fry until golden brown on both sides. Transfer the fish to a platter and keep warm until the sauce is ready.

Ginger sauce
6 dried mushrooms
5 tablespoonsful vinegar
½ teaspoonful salt
¾ cup water
2 tablespoonsful soy sauce
4 tablespoonsful sugar
2 tablespoonsful spring onion, finely chopped
4 tablespoonsful pickled red ginger, chopped
1 tablespoonful cornflour

Soak the mushrooms in hot water for about 40 minutes. Drain away the water and slice finely. In a saucepan combine the vinegar, salt, water, soy sauce, sugar and mushrooms. Bring slowly to the boil and continue boiling until the sugar has dissolved. Add the spring onion and chopped red ginger. Using a little cold water mix the cornflour to a smooth paste. Add it to the sauce and stir over a low heat until the sauce thickens. Remove from the heat and pour over the fish. Garnish with coriander leaves and serve immediately.

Serves 3–4

Ikan Bali (Fish the Balinese Way)

A great deal of fish is eaten in Indonesia. This is one of many fish recipes that have a distinctively Indonesian flavour.

1½ lb (680 g) bass or herring
1 teaspoonful fresh ginger, finely chopped
3 cloves garlic, finely chopped

½ medium onion, finely chopped
2 red chillies, chopped
½ oz (14 g) tamarind
peanut oil for deep frying
1 tablespoonful soy sauce
½ teaspoonful brown sugar
½ teaspoonful salt

Wash the fish and clean it thoroughly. Cut the fish into steaks.
Using a pestle and mortar or an electric blender grind the ginger,
garlic, onion and chillies to a smooth paste. Bring the tamarind to
the boil in a quarter cup of hot water, mash with a fork, remove
from the heat and allow to get cold. Rub the fish steaks with the
tamarind pulp and leave covered for half an hour. In a small pan
heat two tablespoonsful of oil and fry the ground ingredients in it.
Add the soy sauce, brown sugar, salt and a quarter cup of water.
Bring to the boil and simmer for 2–3 minutes only. Once the sauce
is ready pat the fish dry with kitchen paper and deep fry a couple of
pieces at a time until golden brown. Drain on paper. Arrange the
fish on a serving plate and pour the sauce over just before serving.

Serves 4

Mo Hin Gha

This traditional Burmese dish is made using the tender shoots of
the banana tree. The young shoot is peeled of its outermost layers,
cut into thin slices, soaked overnight in salted water and cooked
until tender. Unfortunately banana shoots are hard to obtain
outside the tropics. My Burmese friend suggested that using
bamboo shoots instead would produce a result that is satisfactory
though not entirely authentic. If you are lucky enough to live in a
tropical or sub-tropical country, however, replace the bamboo
shoots by 8 oz (226 g) cooked banana shoots.

5 large onions, finely chopped
9 cloves garlic, chopped
4 teaspoonsful fresh ginger, finely chopped
1½ lb (680 g) filleted herring or mackerel
4 cups hot water
8 tablespoonsful sesame oil
2 teaspoonsful salt
1½ teaspoonsful turmeric powder

1 teaspoonful chilli powder
1 stalk lemon grass or 1 teaspoonful grated lemon rind
2 teaspoonsful dried shrimp paste
2 tablespoonsful fish sauce (nam pla)
7 oz (198 g) creamed coconut
3 tablespoonsful chick pea flour
7 oz (198 g) can bamboo shoots
3 tablespoonsful lemon juice

Using either an electric blender or a pestle and mortar, grind the onions, garlic and ginger to a smooth purée. Wash the fish and boil it for 3 minutes in two of the cups of hot water. Remove the fish and reserve the stock. Heat the oil in a large pan. Add the puréed ingredients and the salt and stir fry for about 5 minutes over a medium heat. Add the fish stock, the turmeric, chilli powder, lemon grass or lemon rind, dried shrimp paste and fish sauce. Dissolve the creamed coconut in the rest of the hot water and add it to the pan. Mix the chick pea flour to a smooth paste in a little cold water, add it to the pan and bring to the boil. Just prior to serving add the fish, diced bamboo shoots and lemon juice to the boiling liquid. Serve hot with extra-fine egg noodles or rice sticks and accompaniments as for Panthay Kaukswe on pp. 81–2.

The guests help themselves to noodles, pour over some fish soup and sprinkle the dish with various garnishes to suit individual tastes.

Serves 6–8

Thai Fried Shrimp and Broccoli

A truly unusual shellfish and vegetable side dish.

8 oz (226 g) prawns
8 oz (226 g) broccoli spears
2 tablespoonsful vegetable oil
4 cloves garlic, chopped
2 teaspoonsful fish sauce (nam pla)

Shell and de-vein the prawns, wash thoroughly and cut each prawn lengthwise into two. Wash and cut the broccoli into bite-sized pieces and soak in ice-cold water for about 10 minutes. In a frying pan heat the oil and fry the garlic until golden brown. Add the prawns and stir fry for about 4 minutes. Add the fish sauce and lastly the drained broccoli and cook for about 5 minutes over a medium heat. The broccoli should be barely cooked and should retain a lovely green colour.

Serves 2–3

Gule Ikan

Fish curry – Indonesian style!

$1\frac{1}{2}$ *lb (680 g) mackerel, tuna or kingfish*
1 teaspoonful fresh ginger, finely chopped
3 cloves garlic, finely chopped
$\frac{1}{2}$ *medium onion, finely chopped*
2 oz (56 g) creamed coconut
$\frac{1}{2}$ *oz (14 g) tamarind*
2 red chillies, chopped
$\frac{1}{4}$ *teaspoonful turmeric*
1 teaspoonful salt
1 stalk lemon grass or $\frac{1}{2}$ teaspoonful grated lemon rind

Wash and clean the fish. Cut into fairly thick steaks. Using a pestle and mortar or an electric blender grind the ginger, garlic and onion to a smooth paste. Dissolve the creamed coconut in half a cup of boiling water. In a pan bring the tamarind and a quarter cup of water to the boil, mash with a fork, remove from the heat and strain. Discard the pulp and reserve the tamarind liquid. In a large shallow pan bring the creamed coconut to the boil. Add the ground ingredients, chilli, turmeric, salt and lemon grass. Add the fish steaks and cook, uncovered, over a low heat, stirring frequently to prevent the gravy curdling. Lastly, add the tamarind water and cook until the fish is done and the gravy is fairly thick. Serve with rice.

Serves 3–4

Fish in Yoghurt Sauce

This is an Indian dish, characteristic of the state of Bengal.

1 lb (454 g) filleted white fish, preferably cod
2 tablespoonsful oil
1 medium onion, chopped

1 teaspoonful fresh ginger, chopped
3 cloves garlic, chopped
½ teaspoonful salt
⅛ teaspoonful turmeric
½ teaspoonful cumin powder
1 teaspoonful coriander powder
½ teaspoonful garam masala
4 fl oz (113 ml) natural unsweetened yoghurt
2 green chillies, chopped

Wash the fish and cut each fillet into two. Heat the oil and fry the onions in it. Add the ginger, garlic, salt and spices. Add the yoghurt and green chillies. Bring to the boil. Reduce the heat and slide in the pieces of fish. Simmer on a low heat for about 15 minutes. Serve with rice.

Serves 2

Red Curry of Shrimp

A Thai speciality, rather hot!

6 red chillies, dried
½ teaspoonful black peppercorns
1 tablespoonful coriander seeds
2 teaspoonsful caraway seeds
1 teaspoonful cumin seeds
1 tablespoonful coriander roots, chopped
1 teaspoonful grated lime or lemon rind
1 teaspoonful salt
1 teaspoonful serai powder
6 cloves garlic
½ medium onion
1 teaspoonful kapi
1 teaspoonful paprika

Using an electric blender begin by grinding all the whole spices until finely ground. Then add the rest of the ingredients and grind to a smooth fine paste.

To make a shrimp curry you need

4 oz (113 g) creamed coconut
1½ cups water
1½ lb (680 g) shrimps or prawns
1 tablespoonful fish sauce (nam pla)
3 tablespoonsful curry paste

In a pan over a low heat dissolve the creamed coconut in the water. If using fresh prawns shell, de-vein and wash them. Once the creamed coconut has dissolved add the shrimps or prawns and bring to the boil. Reduce the heat and simmer for about 12 minutes or until the shrimps are cooked through. Add the rest of the ingredients and simmer for a further 5 minutes. Serve with boiled rice.

Serves 4

Prawn Curry

This is a Sri Lankan recipe. Prawn curry is a luxury even in Sri Lanka, where seafood and shellfish are generally quite plentiful.

1 fl oz (28 ml) vegetable oil
½ medium onion, chopped
5 curry leaves, if available
2 cloves garlic, chopped
½ teaspoonful fresh ginger, chopped
8 oz (226 g) shelled prawns or shrimps
1 in (2.5 cm) piece cinnamon stick
½ teaspoonful turmeric powder
½ teaspoonful fenugreek
½ teaspoonful salt
½ teaspoonful chilli powder
juice of ½ lemon
1 oz (28 g) creamed coconut
4 fl oz (113 ml) water

Heat the oil and fry the onions until they are brown. Add the curry leaves, garlic and ginger and all the ingredients except the creamed coconut and the water. Fry for 5 minutes and then add the creamed coconut and the water. Bring to the boil, cover and simmer for 15 minutes. Serve with rice.

Serves 2–3

Hae Kun (Shrimp Rolls)

A Thai speciality.

2 sheets dried bean curd
1 lb (454 g) shrimps
2 tablespoonsful pork fat, finely chopped

1 teaspoonful salt
2 cloves garlic, finely chopped
$\frac{1}{4}$ teaspoonful freshly milled black pepper
2 tablespoonsful cornflour
oil for frying

Soak the sheets of bean curd in water until they are quite soft.
Clean and wash the shrimps and chop finely. In a bowl mix
together the shrimps, pork fat, salt, garlic, pepper and cornflour.
Divide the mixture into two equal portions. Shape each portion to
resemble a cylindrical roll. Place the shrimp filling on a sheet of
bean curd and roll it up, rather like a long sausage roll. Steam the
rolls for about 10–12 minutes. Allow to cool and cut into $1\frac{1}{2}$ in
(3.7 cm) diagonal slices. Shallow fry in hot oil until brown on both
sides. Drain on paper and serve with sweet and sour sauce (below).

Sweet and sour sauce
6 dried mushrooms
2 tablespoonsful pickled red ginger
6 spring onions
$\frac{1}{4}$ cup sugar
$\frac{1}{2}$ cup vinegar
$\frac{3}{4}$ cup soy sauce
$\frac{1}{4}$ cup water
2 tablespoonsful cornflour

Soak the mushrooms in hot water for 30 minutes. Drain away the
water and chop the mushrooms finely. Finely chop the pickled
ginger. Slice the spring onions. In a pan over a low to medium heat
bring the sugar, vinegar, soy sauce and water to the boil. Allow to
simmer until the sugar has dissolved. Mix the cornflour with a little
water to a smooth paste. Add the mushrooms, ginger and spring
onions to the bubbling sauce. Simmer for 3 minutes. Add the
cornflour and mix thoroughly. Stir over a low heat for about 3
minutes.

Serves 6–8

Sweet and Sour Crab

This is a Singaporean dish which should be prepared with fresh
crabs. The chilli in the dish can be omitted for those who do not
like hot food.

4 fresh crabs
4 tablespoonsful oil
1 medium onion, minced
4 cloves garlic, crushed
3 red chillies, ground
1 stalk lemon grass or ½ teaspoonful grated lemon rind
2 tablespoonsful soy sauce
1 tablespoonful sugar
1 teaspoonful salt
1 tablespoonful vinegar
1 cup water

Wash and clean the crabs. Break away the claws and cut each crab
into four pieces. In a wok or deep frying pan heat the oil. Add the
onion, garlic, chilli and lemon and stir fry for a minute. Add the
crabs and continue to stir fry until they begin to change colour.
Mix the soy sauce, sugar, salt, vinegar and water and add it to the
crabs. Bring to the boil and cook on a medium heat until the sauce
coats the pieces of crab. Serve with white rice.

Serves 4

8

Vegetables

Avial (Mixed Vegetables in Yoghurt Sauce)

This is a kerala (South Indian) speciality and makes an excellent
vegetarian meal. It is traditionally prepared by the South Indian
Tamils.

1 tablespoonful oil
½ teaspoonful turmeric
1 teaspoonful cumin powder
1 tablespoonful coriander powder
3 green chillies, finely chopped
3 cups mixed vegetables cut into bite-sized pieces (e.g. cauliflower, carrots,
     courgettes, aubergines, beans, etc.)
1½ teaspoonsful salt
1½ cups water
1 cup desiccated coconut
1 cup natural unsweetened yoghurt

In a medium sized saucepan heat the oil. Add the spices and
vegetables and lightly toss the vegetables. Add salt and water and
bring to the boil. Lower the heat and simmer for 10 minutes. Add
the coconut and the yoghurt and bring to the boil. Allow to boil for
3 minutes before removing from the heat. Serve with rice.

Serves 4

Sayur Lodeh (Mixed Vegetable Curry)

Indonesia's answer to the well-known South Indian avial (see
recipe).

1 lb (454 g) mixed vegetables (e.g. French beans, courgettes, cauliflower, snow
     peas, aubergine, cabbage, tinned bamboo shoots)
4 oz (113 g) creamed coconut
2 tablespoonsful oil
1 medium onion, finely chopped
1 clove garlic, chopped
½ teaspoonful shrimp paste (trasi)
1 ripe tomato, chopped
¾ teaspoonful salt
¼ teaspoonful brown sugar
2 fresh red chillies, chopped

Wash and cut the beans and courgettes into bite-sized pieces. Cut
the cauliflower into florets. Cut the aubergine into bite-sized cubes.

Shred the cabbage coarsely. Cut the bamboo shoots into small pieces. Dissolve the creamed coconut in 1½ cups of boiling water. In a medium sized pan heat the oil and fry the onion until it is soft. Add the garlic, shrimp paste and tomato. Fry for 1 minute and add half a cup of boiling water to it. Add the coconut milk, salt, sugar and chillies and bring to the boil. Lower the heat to simmer and add the cauliflower florets. After a couple of minutes add the beans, the snow peas (whole) and then the courgettes, aubergines and lastly the cabbage. When the vegetables are cooked without being overcooked, remove from the heat and serve.

Serves 4

Gado-Gado (Mixed Vegetables with a Peanut Sauce)

An Indonesian speciality: a selection of blanched vegetables and hardboiled eggs served with a peanut sauce. The vegetables should not be overcooked and should retain their colour and crispness.

8 oz (226 g) bean sprouts
8 oz (226 g) carrots
8 oz (226 g) French beans
1 small cucumber
½ small cabbage
4 hardboiled eggs
peanut sauce (Sans Katjang) (see BASIC RECIPES*)*

Each vegetable, except the cucumber, should be boiled or blanched separately. Put the bean sprouts into boiling water for a minute. Drain and cool quickly in cold water. Cut the carrots into matchstick-like strips and boil for 3 minutes. String and cut the beans into 1 in (2.5 cm) pieces and blanch for 2 minutes in boiling water. Finely slice the cucumber. Coarsely shred the cabbage and blanch in boiling water for a minute. Cut the hardboiled eggs lengthwise into two. Arrange the cooked vegetables in separate piles, on top of each other, on a large dish. Garnish with the eggs and cucumber slices. Chill in the refrigerator for half an hour before use. Serve with Sans Katjang.

Serves 6–8

Oden

This is a popular Japanese winter dish that is often sold on the streets of Osaka.

1 ×8.82 oz (250 g) tin konnyaku
2 medium carrots
6 oz (168 g) Japanese radish (daikon)
2 pieces fried bean curd (aburagé)
1 fish sausage (kamaboku)
1 sachet (0.3 oz/9 g) dashinomoto
a piece of seaweed (kombu)
1 dessertspoonful sugar
2 tablespoonsful soy sauce
1½ teaspoonsful salt
3 tablespoonsful mirin
12 oz (340 g) bean curd, cut into cubes
6 hardboiled eggs
handful of cabbage leaves, washed
mustard

Cut the konnyaku into large rectangular pieces. Peel and cut the carrots and radish into large pieces. Pour boiling water over the aburagé, drain and cut into bite-sized pieces. Cut the fish sausage into thick slices. In a large pan mix the dashinomoto with five cups of hot water. Add the seaweed, sugar, soy sauce, salt and mirin and bring to the boil. Add the carrot and radish and allow to simmer for 10 minutes, then add the rest of the ingredients and bring to the boil. Simmer gently for about half an hour. To serve ladle into large bowls and eat with mustard.

Serves 6

Sayur Asam (Sour Mixed Vegetables)

An Indonesian speciality, combining several flavours with a spicy seasoning.

8 oz (226 g) stewing beef
a walnut size piece of tamarind
peanut oil for frying
1 medium onion, chopped
3 cloves garlic, chopped
a few curry leaves, if available
½ teaspoonful shrimp paste (trasi) (optional)

1 teaspoonful salt
½ teaspoonful brown sugar
4 oz (113 g) peanuts
2 red chillies, chopped
1 lb (454 g) mixed vegetables (cabbage, beans, aubergine, carrot, corn niblets,
    marrow)

Cut the beef into small pieces. Mash the tamarind in a quarter cup
of boiling water, strain the liquid and reserve. In a medium sized
pan heat a tablespoonful of oil. Add the onion, garlic, meat, curry
leaves and shrimp paste. Stir fry for a couple of minutes. Add two
cups of boiling water, the salt and brown sugar and simmer for half
an hour. Add the peanuts, chillies, tamarind water and the
vegetables. The vegetables that require the most cooking should be
added first and the leafy vegetables for only a minute or two at the
end of the cooking time. Serve hot with rice.

Serves 4–6

Sayur Tumis (Stir Fried Vegetables)

This Indonesian favourite is half way between Indian and Chinese
cooking in character.

3 tablespoonsful oil
1 medium onion, finely chopped
2 cloves garlic, chopped
a few curry leaves, if available
½ teaspoonful shrimp paste (trasi)
1 lb (454 g) mixed vegetables (e.g. French beans, snow peas, aubergine,
    courgettes, cabbage)
½ teaspoonful salt
2 teaspoonsful soy sauce

Heat the oil in a frying pan or wok and cook the onions until soft.
Add the garlic, curry leaves and shrimp paste and stir fry for a
couple of minutes. Now add the vegetables, and stir fry until they
are just cooked. Lastly add the salt and soy sauce and serve
immediately. The vegetables that require the most cooking should
be added first.

Serves 4

Stir Fried Cabbage

This is a really simple method of cooking vegetables to retain their
flavour, crispness and colour. Any green leafy vegetable can be
substituted for Chinese cabbage. It is important to cook the
vegetables on a high heat for a very short time, stirring constantly.

1 lb (454 g) Chinese cabbage
3 tablespoonsful vegetable oil
¾ teaspoonful salt
1 tablespoonful soy sauce
½ teaspoonful sugar
2 teaspoonsful wine vinegar

Wash the cabbage and allow to drain. Cut the cabbage into even-
sized pieces about 1–2 in (2.5–5.0 cm) square. Heat the oil in a wok
or large frying pan over a medium to high flame until it is
smoking. Add the cabbage and stir constantly for 2 minutes. Add
the rest of the ingredients at once and stir fry for a further 1–2
minutes.

Serves 4–6

Stir Fried Spinach

An Indian vegetable dish with a Chinese touch! Spring cabbage can
be substituted for the spinach with the omission of the tomatoes.

1 tablespoonful oil
1 onion, chopped
1 teaspoonful cumin powder
½ teaspoonful coriander powder
½ teaspoonful salt
1 lb (454 g) spinach, chopped
2 ripe tomatoes, chopped

Heat the oil and gently fry the onion in it. Add the spices and salt
and the chopped spinach a little at a time and continue to stir.
Finally add the tomatoes and cook uncovered for 3 minutes.

Serves 4

Stir Fried Snow Peas with Mushrooms

Another Chinese vegetable dish in the stir fried style.

8 Chinese dried mushrooms
1 lb (454 g) snow peas
1 tablespoonful oil
¾ teaspoonful salt
1 tablespoonful soy sauce

Soak the mushrooms in warm water for half an hour. Discard the stems and slice the caps fairly thickly. Snap off the tips of the peas and string them. Heat the oil in a wok or frying pan over a medium to high flame until it is smoking. Add the mushrooms and stir constantly for 2 minutes. Add the peas and the soy sauce and continue to stir fry for a further 2 minutes. Serve at once.

Serves 4

Ghaw-be-thot (Fried Cabbage)

This Burmese cabbage dish is rather salty. If the fishy flavour does not appeal to you, omit the fish sauce.

1 lb (454 g) cabbage
2 tablespoonsful vegetable oil
4 cloves garlic, finely sliced
1 medium onion, finely chopped
2 tablespoonsful dried prawn powder
a pinch of ajinomoto
1 tablespoonful fish sauce (nam pla)

Wash and finely shred the cabbage. In a wok or deep frying pan heat the oil over a medium heat. Add the garlic and fry until pale brown. Add the onions and the dried prawn powder and continue to fry until the onions are softened. Add the cabbage and stir fry for about 5 minutes. Finally add the ajinomoto and the fish sauce and allow to cook for a further 3 minutes.

Serves 4–6

Pisang Goreng (Fried Banana)

These Indonesian fried bananas are served as a snack or as a side dish to a main meal.

6 large ripe bananas
4 tablespoonsful brown sugar
juice of 1 lemon
oil for deep frying

Peel the bananas and slice each lengthwise into two. Sprinkle the bananas with the sugar and lemon juice and leave covered for half an hour. Over a medium flame heat the oil until it is smoking hot. Fry the bananas a few at a time. Drain on kitchen paper.

Serves 6

Spicy Stuffed Cauliflower

An Indian speciality, suitable as a starter or a side dish to a main course.

2 tablespoonsful desiccated coconut
½ cup cooked green peas
½ teaspoonful salt
juice of ½ lemon
1 teaspoonful cumin powder
½ teaspoonful chilli powder
1 green chilli
1 medium cauliflower
1 tablespoonful chopped coriander leaves, for garnishing
4 large lettuce leaves, for garnishing

Blend all the ingredients except the cauliflower, the coriander leaves and the lettuce. Remove the outer leaves from the cauliflower. Cut the main stem so that the cauliflower remains stable when placed on a plate. Cook the cauliflower gently in boiling water until just tender, about 15 minutes. Remove from the pan and place head downwards on a plate. Fill the crevices of the cauliflower with the spicy coconut mixture, taking care that the cauliflower does not disintegrate. Place the cauliflower on a bed of lettuce. Sprinkle with chopped coriander leaves. Serve at room temperature.

Serves 4

Black-eyed Beans

A nourishing and tasty Indian speciality, this dry curry is best served with a rice dish.

8 oz (226 g) black-eyed beans
1 tablespoonful cooking oil
½ medium onion, finely chopped
¼ teaspoonful turmeric powder
1 teaspoonful cumin powder
½ teaspoonful coriander powder
½ teaspoonful garam masala
1 teaspoonful salt
coriander leaves, for garnishing

Wash and soak the beans in cold water for 2 hours. Put the beans in a pan with three-quarters of a cup of water and bring to the boil. Lower the heat and simmer until all the water is absorbed. In another pan heat the oil and fry the onions until golden brown. Add the spices, salt and lastly the beans and stir over a low heat for about a minute. Garnish with coriander leaves and serve with chappatis or rice.

Serves 4–6

Curried Aubergines

This recipe is common in India and Sri Lanka, combining the delicate flavour of aubergines with coconut and spices.

2 oz (56 g) creamed coconut
4 fl oz (113 ml) water
2 green chillies, chopped
a few curry leaves
1 medium onion, finely chopped
1½ fl oz (42 ml) malt vinegar
1 teaspoonful sugar
½ dessertspoonful mustard
1½ teaspoonsful coriander
1½ teaspoonsful cumin powder
1 in (2.5 cm) piece of cinnamon
¼ teaspoonful turmeric
1 teaspoonful salt
1 lb (454 g) aubergines, cut into ½ in (1.25 cm) cubes and deep fried until
    golden brown

Allow the creamed coconut to dissolve in the water over a low heat. Add all the ingredients except the aubergines to the dissolved creamed coconut and cook for 7 minutes. Once this sauce is thick add the aubergines and simmer for a further 5 minutes.

Serves 4

Stuffed Bhindi (Okra or Lady's Fingers)

A North Indian speciality, in which bhindi are slit and stuffed with
a spicy coconut filling.

3 oz (85 g) desiccated coconut
1 teaspoonful salt
½ teaspoonful cumin powder
¼ teaspoonful chilli powder
¼ teaspoonful turmeric powder
juice of ½ lemon
1 lb (454 g) bhindi
3 fl oz (85 ml) oil

In a bowl mix all the ingredients except the bhindi. Slit each bhindi
lengthwise and carefully force in a small quantity of the coconut
filling. In a large frying pan heat the oil. Carefully arrange the
bhindis in the frying pan and allow to cook for 5 minutes. Turn
each bhindi over and cook for a further 5 minutes, adding more
cooking oil if necessary.

Serves 4

Cashewnut Curry

This is a tasty Sri Lankan favourite and could be used as the main
source of protein for a vegetarian meal. It combines an unusual
texture and flavour.

8 oz (226 g) cashewnuts
1 tablespoonful oil
1 medium onion, finely chopped
1½ teaspoonsful coriander powder
1 teaspoonful cumin powder
¼ teaspoonful turmeric
2 cloves
2 cardamoms
2 pieces cinnamon stick
1 teaspoonful salt
1 oz (28 g) creamed coconut

Add half a teaspoonful of bicarbonate of soda to three cups of cold
water and soak the cashewnuts in this for 8 hours. Drain away the
water. In a pan heat the oil and fry the onions until lightly

browned. Add the spices, salt and cashewnuts and mix thoroughly. Add the creamed coconut and half a cup of water and bring to the boil. Lower the heat and simmer for 15 minutes.

Serves 3–4

Parippu (Lentil Curry)

Lentils are rich in protein and make for an excellent meat substitute in India and Sri Lanka. To vary the flavour, a small can of tomatoes can be added before the final simmering.

1½ cups masur lentils (the orange lentil)
1 medium onion, finely shredded
2 tablespoonsful oil
¼ teaspoonful mustard seeds
2 green chillies, chopped
a few curry leaves (optional)
1 teaspoonful cumin powder
1 teaspoonful coriander powder
¼ teaspoonful turmeric powder
¼ teaspoonful fenugreek seeds
2 teaspoonsful salt

Wash the lentils in a sieve under running water. Put in a pan with three cups of water and half the onion and boil slowly until the lentils are cooked and quite mushy. In another pan heat the oil and splutter the mustard seeds in it. Fry the remainder of the onions until golden brown. Add the rest of the spices and lastly the lentils. Allow to simmer for 15 minutes.

Serves 6

Thur Dhal

This Indian preparation is made from a substantial meat substitute. It is excellent served with a rice dish.

1½ cups thur lentils
1 tablespoonful oil
¼ teaspoonful mustard seed
a pinch of asafoetida (optional)
3 cloves garlic, chopped

$\frac{1}{4}$ teaspoonful turmeric powder
1 teaspoonful salt
$\frac{1}{2}$ oz (14 g) tamarind dissolved in 2 fl oz (56 ml) boiling water
2 green chillies, chopped
6 fl oz (170 ml) water

Wash and soak the lentils overnight in three cups of water. Cook the lentils in three cups of water for 35 minutes. In another pan heat the oil and splutter the mustard seeds in it. Add the garlic and fry for 3 minutes. Add the spices, salt and the strained tamarind water. Finally add the lentils, green chillies and water and bring to the boil. Simmer for 5 minutes.

Serves 6

Moong Dhal with Spinach

$1\frac{1}{2}$ cups yellow moong dhal
2 tablespoonsful oil
$\frac{1}{4}$ teaspoonful mustard seed
5 curry leaves, if available
1 teaspoonful fresh ginger, chopped
$\frac{1}{4}$ teaspoonful turmeric powder
1 teaspoonful cumin powder
$1\frac{1}{2}$ teaspoonsful salt
2 tablespoonsful spring onions, chopped
2 green chillies, chopped
4 oz (113 g) spinach, chopped

Wash the lentils and bring to the boil with three cups of water. Cover and simmer for about 30 minutes. In another pan heat the oil, add the mustard seeds and allow to splutter. Add the curry leaves, the ginger and the spices. Fry for a few minutes. Add the salt and the spring onions and green chillies and pour in the boiled lentils. Bring to the boil and cook for 5 minutes. Lastly add the chopped spinach and allow to simmer for about 5 minutes. Serve with rice or chappatis.

Serves 6

Leeks in Gram Flour

A North Indian speciality.

1 tablespoonful oil
$\frac{1}{4}$ teaspoonful mustard seeds
$\frac{1}{4}$ teaspoonful chilli powder
$\frac{1}{4}$ teaspoonful turmeric powder
$\frac{1}{2}$ teaspoonful salt
1 lb (454 g) leeks cut into 1 in (2.5 cm) pieces
$\frac{3}{4}$ cup water
1 oz (28 g) gram flour

Heat the oil, add the mustard seeds and allow to splutter. Add the rest of the spices and lastly the leeks. Toss the leeks for a few seconds in the pan. Add the water, bring to the boil and allow the leeks to cook over a low heat (about 5 minutes). In a bowl mix the gram flour with sufficient water to make a stiff paste. Take the pan off the heat and work the gram flour paste into the leeks. When mixed thoroughly return to a low heat and allow to cook for 5 minutes.

Serves 3

9

Salads

Onion Salad

A popular accompaniment to an Indian main course.

8 oz (226 g) onions
juice of 1 lemon
½ teaspoonful salt
2 green chillies, finely chopped
¼ teaspoonful freshly milled black pepper

Finely slice the onions, using a cucumber slicer if available. Add all the ingredients and leave for at least 1 hour before serving. Before serving finely sliced tomatoes can be added.

Serves 4

Lettuce with Peanut Dressing

An excellent Indian salad to accompany a dry curry and a rice dish.

2 fl oz (56 ml) oil
¼ teaspoonful mustard seeds
¼ teaspoonful cumin seeds
a pinch of turmeric
½ teaspoonful salt
1 fl oz (28 ml) lemon juice
1 lettuce, washed and dried
½ cucumber, sliced
2 oz (56 g) peanuts, coarsely ground

Heat oil and splutter the mustard seeds in it. Add the cumin seeds, turmeric and salt. Remove from the heat and add the lemon juice. Allow the dressing to get cold before tossing into the other salad ingredients.

Serves 4

Liang-pan-huang-kua (Chinese Cucumber Salad)

This cucumber salad with its spicy dressing is a good side dish for a Chinese meal.

2 medium cucumbers
1 teaspoonful soy sauce
1 tablespoonful wine vinegar

2 teaspoonsful sesame oil
1 tablespoonful sugar
$\frac{1}{4}$ teaspoonful chilli powder
$\frac{1}{2}$ teaspoonful salt

Peel the cucumbers and cut them in half lengthwise. Scoop out the seeds and slice the peeled cucumber halves into $\frac{1}{8}$ in (3 mm) slices. In a bowl combine the cucumber slices, the soy sauce, wine vinegar, sesame oil, sugar, chilli powder and salt, and mix well. Chill before serving.

Serves 4

Thai Cucumber Salad

This dish should be prepared just prior to serving.

3 tender green cucumbers
$\frac{1}{2}$ small onion
2–3 fresh red chillies
$2\frac{1}{2}$ tablespoonsful dried prawn powder
1 tablespoonful lime or lemon juice
1 tablespoonful fish sauce (nam pla)

Grate the cucumbers. Finely chop the onion. Slice the red chillies. In a bowl mix all the ingredients together and serve immediately.

Serves 4–6

Selada Tomat

Indonesian tomato salad. This is an excellent accompaniment to a rice dish.

4 ripe tomatoes
salt to taste
2 green chillies
3 tablespoonsful sugar
juice of 2 lemons

Slice the tomatoes and arrange at the base of a serving platter. Sprinkle with salt. Slice the green chillies slantwise and arrange over the tomato slices. Sprinkle the sugar and lemon juice over the salad and allow to stand for an hour or two before serving.

Serves 4

Thai Vegetable Salad

Winged beans are used in this salad, but parboiled French beans or snow peas can be substituted when winged beans are unavailable.

8 oz (226 g) winged beans or French beans or snow peas
2 oz (56 g) creamed coconut
2 oz (56 g) desiccated coconut
½ oz (14 g) lard
2 oz (56 g) lean pork, finely sliced
2 tablespoonsful dried prawn powder
1 teaspoonful palm sugar
1 tablespoonful fish sauce (nam pla)
1 tablespoonful nam prik (see BASIC RECIPES)
2 red chillies, finely sliced
1 tablespoonful lime or lemon juice
2 tablespoonsful roasted peanuts, coarsely ground

Wash and parboil the beans in a little water. In a pan, over a low heat, dissolve the creamed coconut in a quarter cup of water. In a heavy bottomed pan over a medium heat roast the desiccated coconut until pale brown. Care should be taken to prevent the coconut from burning. Heat the lard and over a medium to high heat fry the pork until cooked through. Add the prawn powder, sugar, fish sauce and nam prik and mix thoroughly. Remove from the heat and allow to get cold. Just prior to serving in a large bowl combine all the ingredients and mix thoroughly.

Serves 4–6

Thai Raw Mango Salad

When green mangoes are not readily available, you could use tart eating apples or cooking apples for this typical Thai salad.

2 firm raw green mangoes
1 teaspoonful salt
1 tablespoonful lard or vegetable oil
3 cloves garlic, finely sliced
5 spring onions, cut into ½ in (1.25 cm) pieces
6 oz (168 g) lean pork, finely sliced
1 tablespoonful dried prawn powder
1 tablespoonful roasted peanuts, coarsely ground
1 tablespoonful fish sauce (nam pla)
1 teaspoonful palm sugar

Peel and finely slice the mangoes. Sprinkle with the salt and leave for 5 minutes. Wash the mango slices and pat dry on kitchen paper. Heat the oil and over a medium heat fry the garlic until pale brown. Remove the garlic and add the spring onions to the hot oil. Fry for about 1 minute and remove from the pan. In the same oil fry the pork until cooked through. Add the prawn powder, peanuts, nam pla and sugar and mix thoroughly. Remove from the heat and allow to get cold. Just prior to serving combine all the ingredients in a large bowl.

Serves 4–6

Hsia-mi-pan Ch'in-ts'ai

This Chinese celery and dried shrimp salad dish is an excellent accompaniment to a Chinese meal.

2 oz (56 g) Chinese dried shrimps
1 tablespoonful Chinese rice wine or dry sherry
1 tablespoonful warm water
1 head celery
1 teaspoonful soy sauce
1 tablespoonful wine vinegar
2 teaspoonsful sesame oil
1 tablespoonful sugar
½ teaspoonful salt

Wash the shrimps thoroughly under cold running water. Mix the wine and warm water in a bowl. Add the shrimps and allow to marinade for half an hour. Drain so as to save the marinade. Cut the celery crosswise into 1 in (2.5 cm) pieces. In a large bowl combine the marinade, the soy sauce, vinegar, sesame oil, sugar and salt and stir thoroughly until the sugar dissolves. Mix in the celery and shrimps, tossing until all the pieces are well coated with the dressing. Chill before serving.

Serves 4

Selada Udang

Indonesian prawn salad.

2 large potatoes, boiled in jackets and peeled
8 oz (226 g) cooked shelled prawns

4 oz (113 g) French beans, stringed, cut into 2 in (5 cm) lengths and boiled
1 medium lettuce, washed
mayonnaise
salt to taste

Slice the potatoes into $\frac{1}{8}$ in (3 mm) slices. Arrange the potato slices, prawns, beans and lettuce leaves on a platter. Serve with mayonnaise and salt to taste.

Serves 4

Tahu Goreng (Spicy Bean Curd Salad)

This delicious bean curd salad with spicy peanut sauce is an Indonesian speciality. It is an excellent starter to a Far Eastern meal.

2 fresh chillies, de-seeded and finely chopped
3 cloves garlic, crushed
4 oz (113 g) crunchy peanut butter
1 tablespoonful brown sugar
2 tablespoonsful soy sauce
1 tablespoonful vinegar
$\frac{1}{4}$ teaspoonful salt
$\frac{1}{2}$ cup water
8 oz (226 g) bean curd
2 oz (56 g) bean sprouts
1 small cucumber, finely sliced
oil for frying

In a medium saucepan combine all the ingredients except the bean curd, bean sprouts and cucumber. Bring to the boil over a low heat stirring constantly, and allow to cool.

Cut the bean curd into cubes and deep fry until evenly browned. Spread the sliced cucumber on a platter and then arrange the bean curd over it. Bring a pan of water to the boil, add the bean sprouts to it and bring back to the boil, drain in a colander adding cold water to cool. Arrange the bean sprouts on the platter. Finally pour the peanut sauce over the salad.

Serves 4

Selada Husar (Beef with Pineapple Salad)

Indonesian Hussar salad: a salad for aristocrats!

1 lb (454 g) roast beef, sliced
1 small ripe pineapple, peeled and sliced
2 tart green apples, peeled, cored and sliced
6 potatoes, peeled, sliced and fried
2 cucumbers, peeled and sliced slantwise
1 red pepper, sliced
3 large carrots, boiled and grated
2 pickled beetroots, sliced
10 lettuce leaves

Sauce
5 eggs, hardboiled and shelled
2 oz (56 g) butter
salt and pepper to taste
1 teaspoonful sugar
mustard to taste
vinegar

Make the sauce first. Separate the egg yolks from the whites and reserve the whites. Cream the butter, and add salt, pepper, sugar and mustard to taste. Add the egg yolks one at a time and mash well to make a smooth mixture. Mix with vinegar to obtain a thick dressing.

Line a platter with the lettuce leaves. Arrange the other salad ingredients in an attractive manner and garnish with the chopped egg whites. Serve with the sauce.

Serves 4

Cha-yeh-tan (Tea-leaf Eggs)

This dish takes a long time to prepare, but it is very attractive as an hors d'oeuvre or a side dish in a Chinese meal.

6 eggs
water as required
2 teaspoonsful salt
1 star anise (whole)
2 teaspoonsful black tea
2 tablespoonsful soy sauce

In a saucepan cover the eggs with about a pint of cold water. Bring to the boil and simmer for 25 minutes. Leave to cool. Now pour off the water and tap each egg gently over its surface with a spoon so that it becomes covered with a mesh of very fine cracks. Place the eggs back in the saucepan together with 1 pint (568 ml) cold water, salt, star anise, tea and soy sauce. Bring rapidly to the boil and then simmer at the very lowest heat for 2 hours. Note that the eggs should be covered with water throughout. Check periodically and top up the pan with boiling water as required. Allow to cool in the liquid for at least 8 hours. Before serving remove the egg shells. The eggs will be covered with a mesh of fine dark lines. Cut in halves and arrange on a platter.

Serves 3

Telur Asin (Salted Eggs)

This Indonesian preparation is not quite as exotic as Chinese hundred-year-old eggs, but it is just as interesting.

10 eggs, preferably duck
4 cups boiling water
1¼ cups salt

Boil the eggs in water for 7 minutes making sure that none of the shells have any cracks on them. In a non-metallic jar or container mix the salt and the boiling water. Allow the salt water and eggs to cool thoroughly. Add the eggs to the salt water making sure that they are all immersed in the water. Leave covered for three weeks. Shell the eggs, halve them and serve with rice.

Serves 5

10

Sweets

Watermelon filled with Fruit

A deliciously refreshing Chinese dessert.

1 medium sized ripe watermelon
1 can lychees
1 can loquats
1 can mandarin segments
1 honeydew or canteloupe melon

Cut the watermelon crosswise into two. Discard the seeds and pulp and scoop out the flesh using a melon baller. Drain the lychees, loquats and mandarins. Cut the honeydew or canteloupe melon into two and, using the melon baller, scoop out the flesh. Arrange the segments of fruit attractively in one of the watermelon shells. Chill thoroughly before serving.

Serves 6–8

Es Krim Adpokat (Avocado Ice Cream)

This Indonesian style ice cream has an unusual flavour and is well worth a try!

6 ripe avocados
2 tablespoonsful instant coffee
1 tablespoonful hot water
1 pint (568 ml) evaporated milk
12 oz (350 g) castor sugar
1 teaspoonful vanilla essence

Cut the avocados in half. Scoop out the flesh and mash with a fork. Dissolve the coffee in the hot water. In a blender mix together the milk, sugar, fruit, coffee and essence. Pour the mixture into ice trays and freeze until almost set. Remove from the freezer and whisk the mixture until frothy. Refreeze and serve when set.

Serves 4–6

Awayuki Kan (Japanese Jelly)

A refreshing Japanese summer dessert, popular with children.

0.15 oz (5 g) agar agar
3 cups cold water

1 cup sugar
2 egg whites
8 oz (226 g) strawberries

Soak the agar agar in the cold water for at least 4 hours. Bring slowly to the boil and continue to simmer until the agar agar strands are dissolved. Add the sugar and allow the mixture to get cold. Beat the egg whites until stiff and add the liquid mixture a little at a time, continuing to beat the egg whites until all the liquid mixture has been incorporated into the egg whites. Rinse out a shallow rectangular dish in cold water and pour the jelly into it. Decorate with the strawberries. Allow to set and cut into large squares.

Serves 6

Chow-Chaw (Agar Agar the Burmese Way)

0.3 oz (10 g) agar agar
$5\frac{1}{2}$ cups cold water
$1\frac{1}{2}$ cups sugar
7 oz (198 g) creamed coconut
a few drops of red food colouring
rose water to flavour

Soak the agar agar in the water for at least 4 hours. Bring slowly to the boil and continue to simmer until the agar agar strands have dissolved. Add the sugar and the creamed coconut and stir until the coconut has dissolved. Remove from the heat and add the red colouring and sufficient rose water to give a mild rose flavour. Pour into shallow rectangular dishes which have just been rinsed in cold water. When set cut into diamond shapes and serve.

Serves 6

Almond Jelly

Agar agar is a type of seaweed and, unlike gelatine, has setting properties that do not need refrigeration. It is colourless and flavourless and sets to a superb solid texture which can be easily cut into cubes. This Chinese dessert can be eaten plain or with any canned fruit, and is particularly delicious with lychees.

0.3 oz (10 g) agar agar (available from Chinese supermarkets)
6½ cups cold water
14 fl oz (414 ml) milk
12 oz (340 g) sugar
2½ teaspoonsful concentrated almond essence

Using a pair of scissors snip the strips of agar agar into 1 in (2.5 cm) pieces. In a large bowl soak the agar agar in the water for about 8 hours. Bring the agar agar and water to the boil in a pan. Simmer until dissolved. Add the rest of the ingredients and boil for a further 10 minutes. Remove from the heat and set in two shallow dishes approximately 14 ×6 ×2 in (36 × 15 × 5 cm). When set cut into cubes and pile onto individual serving dishes.

Serves 6

Agar Agar Serikaya

This Malaysian preparation is a delicious, attractive and refreshing coconut-flavoured jelly.

0.3 oz (10 g) agar agar
7 cups cold water
6 oz (168 g) creamed coconut
11 oz (310 g) soft dark brown sugar (or gula melaka)
¼ teaspoonful nutmeg, grated

Using a pair of scissors snip the strips of agar agar into 1 in (2.5 cm) pieces. In a large bowl soak the agar agar in the water for about 8 hours. Bring the agar agar to the boil in a pan and simmer until dissolved. Add the creamed coconut and the sugar and stir continuously until dissolved. Add the grated nutmeg and boil for a further 5 minutes. Pour into a glass bowl and allow to cool. Chill in refrigerator.

Serves 6

Kluay Chap (Chipped Bananas in Sugar Syrup)

This is a popular Thai way of using bananas. The chipped bananas can be stored in an airtight container for several weeks. Breadfruit can be treated in a similar way.

2 large ripe but firm bananas weighing about 1 lb (454 g)
3 tablespoonsful lemon or lime juice
1 cup cold water
oil for deep frying
½ cup granulated sugar
¾ cup water

Peel and very finely slice the bananas. In a bowl mix the lemon or lime juice with the cup of cold water. Put the sliced bananas into this lemon solution to prevent discolouring. Heat the oil until very hot. Deep fry the banana slices a few at a time until brown and crisp. Care should be taken to drain away as much of the soaking solution as possible and only to fry a few slices at a time to prevent them sticking together.

In a saucepan combine the sugar and the three-quarter cup of water. Stir over a low heat until the sugar has dissolved, then boil rapidly until the solution is thick and syrupy. Add all the banana chips at once and stir over a medium heat for about 2 minutes or until the chips are coated with the sugar syrup. Cool before serving.

Serves 2–3

Kluay Chuam (Stewed Bananas the Thai Way)

1 cup granulated sugar
1½ cups water
5–6 ripe but firm bananas, about 2 lb (900 g) in weight

In a heavy bottomed pan combine the sugar and water. Dissolve the sugar over a low heat. Bring to the boil. Add the bananas, having cut each one crosswise into two. Cook uncovered until the bananas look translucent. Serve hot either plain or with a sauce made by dissolving 4 oz (113 g) creamed coconut in a cup of hot water to which a pinch of salt has been added.

Serves 4

Khanom Talai (Layered Steamed Blancmange)

This is a popular Thai sweet which is similar in texture to blancmange. The Thais use scented water to flavour the sweet. The colour and flavour contrast between the sweet brown bottom layer and the white salty top layer is interesting.

8 oz (226 g) creamed coconut
4 tablespoonsful dark brown sugar
2 tablespoonsful glutinous rice flour
¾ teaspoonful salt
1 teaspoonful rose water

In a pan over a low heat dissolve half the creamed coconut in 1½ cups of hot water. Add the sugar and allow to cool. Mix the flour with a quarter cup of cold water to form a smooth paste. Add the flour to the liquid mixture. Pour into a bowl or individual cups and steam until set. While the bottom layer is steaming combine half a tablespoonful of glutinous rice flour with two tablespoonsful cold water. In a pan over a low heat dissolve the remaining creamed coconut in a cup of hot water. Allow to cool. Add the flour paste, the salt and the rose water and mix. Once the bottom layer has set, carefully pour over the thick white mixture. Resteam until set. Serve hot or cold.

Serves 4

Khanom Sai Kai (Saffron Flavoured Fritters)

A subtly flavoured Thai dessert, these delicious fritters are ideal after any spicy main course. Care should be taken to get regular spherical shapes.

¾ teaspoonful saffron
4 oz (113 g) creamed coconut
¾ cup boiling water
8 oz (226 g) plain white flour
½ teaspoonful bicarbonate of soda
a pinch of salt
oil for deep frying
8 oz (226 g) sugar
¼ cup water

Soak the saffron in one tablespoonful of hot water. Over a low flame dissolve the creamed coconut in the boiling water. Sift the flour into a bowl. Add the bicarbonate of soda and the salt. Once the creamed coconut has cooled, gradually stir it into the flour to form a very stiff batter – stiff enough to be of a dropping consistency. If the batter is too stiff for dropping into hot oil, add a little cold water. Add the saffron and beat until smooth and elastic.

Heat the oil over a medium heat. Drop teaspoonsful of the batter into the hot oil. Allow to fry until evenly browned on both sides. Drain on kitchen paper.

In a pan combine the sugar and the quarter cup of water. Stir over a low heat until the sugar has dissolved, then bring rapidly to the boil. Once this liquid is syrupy keep it warm on a very low heat. Dip the warm fritters into the syrup and drain on kitchen paper.

Makes 30–40, serves 6–8

The Eight Treasure Rice Dessert

A Chinese dessert suitable for a feast!

6 oz (168 g) short grain rice
1⅓ cups water
2 oz (56 g) sugar
1 oz (28 g) melted lard
2 oz (56 g) stoned dates, chopped
2 oz (56 g) red and green glacé cherries
2 oz (56 g) canned red bean paste
1 oz (28 g) blanched whole almonds
1 oz (28 g) walnut pieces

Wash the rice in a sieve under running cold water until the water that runs is clear. Put the rice and water into a medium sized pan and bring rapidly to the boil. Lower the heat so as just to simmer. Place the lid on and cook for 15 minutes until the water has been absorbed. Mix in the sugar and the melted lard. Lightly grease a 2 pint (1.2 l) pudding bowl. Put a layer of rice at the bottom and then add a mixture of the fruit and nuts. Cover with rice. Continue this layering process until the fruit has been used up. Cover with greaseproof paper and steam in a colander over boiling water for 30 minutes. Unmould and serve warm.

Serves 6

Kue Lapis (Layered Rice Flour Cake)

This steamed two-coloured cake is a popular accompaniment to tea or coffee in Indonesia.

12 oz (340 g) rice flour
8 oz (226 g) white sugar
10 oz (280 g) creamed coconut
2 pints (1.2 l) water
2 teaspoonsful vanilla essence
4 drops peanut oil
3–4 drops green food colouring

In a bowl mix the rice flour and the sugar. In a pan over a low heat dissolve the creamed coconut in the water. Add the vanilla essence and the oil to the coconut milk. The milk should be hot but *not* boiling before adding to the flour. Make a well in the centre of the flour and gradually beat the coconut milk to a smooth paste. Divide the mixture into two. Add the colouring to one half and mix thoroughly. Grease a 5 in (13 cm) cake tin and spread half the green dough at the bottom. Steam, covered, in a colander over boiling water for about 40 minutes or until the dough is firm. Lightly grease the cooked layer with oil and place half the white dough and resteam. Repeat the process until the dough is used up. Remove the cake and allow to get cold. Cut into pieces and serve with tea or coffee.

Serves 8–10

Khao Nieo Kaeo (Glutinous Rice Pudding)

This is a Thai version of our rice pudding. Traditionally the rice is soaked in scented water and cooked in coconut milk. It is served with freshly chopped mango or jack fruit, but any fruit can be used.

1 cup glutinous rice
½ teaspoonful salt
2 tablespoonsful rose water
4 oz (113 g) creamed coconut
1½ cups hot water
½ cup sugar

Wash the rice and soak it in two cups of cold water for about 8 hours. Drain away the water. Put the rice, salt, rose water and two cups of fresh cold water into a pan and bring rapidly to the boil. Cover and simmer for 12–15 minutes. Allow to get cold. While the rice is cooling dissolve the creamed coconut in another pan, over a low heat in the hot water. Add the sugar and continue stirring until it has dissolved. Add the cold rice to this boiling sweetened coconut syrup and cook over a low flame for about 5 minutes or until thick. It is important to stir the rice constantly to prevent it sticking to the bottom of the pan. Cool and serve with fresh chopped fruit.

Serves 4–6

Sa-nwin-makin

This popular Burmese cake has an unusual coconut and sesame seed flavour. It is popular with adults and children alike and can be made easily.

1 × 14 fl oz (414 ml) tin evaporated milk
14 fl oz (414 ml) water
8 oz (226 g) sugar
7 oz (198 g) creamed coconut
9 oz (225 g) coarse semolina
3 oz (85 g) butter
3 eggs, separated
½ teaspoonful ground cardamoms
2 tablespoonsful sesame seeds

Combine the milk, water and sugar in a pan and dissolve the creamed coconut in it over a low heat. Put the semolina into a medium sized heavy bottomed pan. Gradually stir in the milk, mixing constantly to prevent any lumps from forming. Add the butter and cook the semolina over a medium heat until all the liquid has evaporated and the mixture resembles a thick paste. Allow to get cold. Beat the egg yolks and mix into the cold semolina. Add the cardamoms. Whisk the egg whites until stiff and fold into the semolina. In a heavy bottomed shallow frying pan dry roast the sesame seeds until evenly browned. Grease a shallow pan approximately 20 × 20 in (50 × 50 cm) and pour the semolina mixture into it. Smooth the top with a knife. Sprinkle generously with the sesame seeds and bake for 50 minutes at Gas Mark 2/300°F or until lightly browned on the top. Allow to get cold and cut into diamond shapes.

Serves 8–10

Lepat Nagasari (Small Banana Cakes)

An Indonesian speciality, these little rice flour cakes are set in cups made of banana leaves. Since banana leaves are hard to come by use small china or glass bowls.

4 large ripe bananas
6 oz (168 g) creamed coconut
1½ pints (852 ml) water
8 oz (226 g) sugar
pinch of salt
1 teaspoonful vanilla essence
1 lb (454 g) rice flour

Place the bananas (unpeeled) in a large pan and cover with cold water. Bring to the boil and simmer for 5 minutes. Allow to cool. In a pan over a low heat dissolve the creamed coconut in the water. Add the sugar, salt, and vanilla essence and cook for a further 5 minutes. Allow to cool slightly. When the coconut milk is warm gradually add the rice flour to it. Care should be taken to beat the dough to prevent any lumps forming. Return the dough to the fire and cook over a low heat until the mixture becomes transparent. Pour a little of the mixture into twelve small individual bowls. Peel and slice each banana into four. Place a slice of banana on each rice flour cake. Serve cold.

Serves 12

Serabi (Rice Flour Patties)

An Indonesian delicacy, these rice flour patties are served with a sauce made of coconut milk.

1 lb (454 g) rice flour
a pinch of salt
8 oz (226 g) desiccated coconut
hot water
7 oz (198 g) creamed coconut
8 oz (226 g) brown sugar
2 teaspoonsful vanilla essence
oil for shallow frying

Put the flour, salt and desiccated coconut into a bowl. Using enough hot but not boiling water, mix the flour to a stiff dough. Allow the dough to stand, covered, for half an hour. To make the coconut sauce, dissolve the creamed coconut in 1 pint (568 ml) of water in a pan over low heat. Add the sugar and vanilla essence and simmer until thick. Heat the oil in a frying pan. Shape the dough to resemble hamburgers and fry a few at a time until golden brown on both sides. Drain on paper. Serve hot with the coconut sauce.

Serves 6–8

Firnee

This Indian rice blancmange is easy to make provided you have the patience to stir it constantly during the cooking time. It is delicately flavoured and popular with adults and children alike.

4 cardamom pods
3 tablespoonsful rice flour
1 pint (568 ml) milk
3 tablespoonsful sugar
3 drops rose essence or 3 tablespoonsful rose water
1½ oz (42 g) chopped almonds

Remove the seeds from the cardamom pods. Using a pestle and mortar or the back of a wooden spoon crush the seeds. Mix the rice flour to a smooth paste with a little of the cold milk. Bring the rest of the milk to the boil and add it gradually to the flour paste. Pour back into the pan and over a low heat, stirring constantly, bring the mixture back to the boil. Add the sugar and allow to simmer for about 5 minutes taking care to stir the mixture constantly so that it remains smooth and free of lumps. Add the cardamoms and the rose water and most of the almonds, reserving enough to sprinkle as a decoration on the top. Serve warm or cold.

Serves 4–5

Mandarin Pancakes

These pancakes are traditionally served with Peking Duck. They should be soft and pliable and can be made in advance and frozen. To reheat simply warm them, covered in foil, in a moderate oven for 10–15 minutes. During every stage of preparation it is important to keep the pancakes covered, to prevent them from drying out.

12 oz (340 g) plain white flour
$\frac{1}{2}$–$\frac{3}{4}$ pint (284–426 ml) boiling water
2–3 tablespoonsful sesame oil

Sift the flour into a mixing bowl. Add a sufficient amount of boiling water to form a soft dough. When the dough is cool enough to handle knead thoroughly until smooth and elastic. Cover with a damp cloth and keep in a cool place for about 20 minutes. On a lightly floured surface roll the dough out to about $\frac{1}{4}$ in (6 mm) thickness. Using a 3 in (7.5 cm) pastry cutter or glass cut out as many circles of dough as you can. Collect the remaining dough, reknead, roll out and cut more circles until all the dough has been used up. While rolling out the dough for the second time, cover the circles of dough with a damp cloth to prevent them drying out.

Brush half the circles of dough with sesame oil. Place a circle of unoiled dough on each one that has been oiled. Evenly roll out each circle of dough to 6–7 in (15–17 cm). Heat a griddle on a medium flame. Cook the pancakes on both sides until speckled. Gently peel the two layers apart. Stack on a plate and leave, covered, until all the pancakes have been cooked.

Makes 30–35, serves 6

Khanom Klok (Thai Pancakes)

These coconut-flavoured pancakes make a welcome change from the normal pancakes. The sugar can be omitted from the batter and the pancakes can be eaten with jam or any other sweet filling.

3 oz (85 g) creamed coconut
6 fl oz (170 ml) hot water
3 fl oz (85 ml) cold water
1 level cupful rice flour (available from Chinese shops)
$\frac{1}{3}$ cup sugar
a pinch of salt
2 eggs, lightly beaten
granulated sugar

In a pan over a low heat dissolve the creamed coconut in the hot water. Add the cold water and allow this mixture to get cool. In a bowl mix the flour, sugar and salt. Add the cooled coconut liquid a little at a time and mix to a stiff batter. Add the eggs and beat until smooth.

Heat a 9 in (23 cm) frying pan over a medium heat. Lightly grease it with oil or lard. Pour two tablespoonsful of the batter into the pan and quickly swirl it around so that a thin layer of the batter covers the surface of the pan. Once the edges of the pancake start to brown lightly flip it over and cook the other side of the pancake for a minute or two. Roll and sprinkle with granulated sugar before serving.

Makes 12, serves 4

Sweet Wontons

These traditional Chinese sweets are well worth trying.

1½ lb (680 g) stoned dates
8 oz (226 g) walnuts, very finely chopped
grated rind of ½ orange
2–3 tablespoonsful orange juice
8 oz (226 g) wonton wrappers (see BASIC RECIPES*)*
oil for deep frying
icing sugar

Mince or chop the dates very finely. In a bowl mix together the dates, walnuts and orange rind. Add a sufficient quantity of orange juice so that the mixture will hold together. Take about a heaped teaspoonful of the date mixture and, using the palms of your hands, firm into a cylindrical shape. Place the date filling diagonally across the centre of the wrapper. Cover the filling with the lower half of the wrapper. Roll up the wrapper so that the filling is encased. Moisten your first finger with cold water and seal the edge. Twist the two ends of the wrapper to resemble a bon-bon or wrapped sweet. Repeat the process until all the filling is used up. Heat the oil until it is smoking hot. Fry the wontons a few at a time until pale brown. Drain on kitchen paper and when cold sprinkle with icing sugar.

Makes 40–50

Watalappan

This is a Sri Lankan dessert that is said to be fit for royalty. Where jaggery is not available 8 oz (226 g) dark brown sugar may be substituted.

8 oz (226 g) jaggery (available at Indian grocery stores)
2 fl oz (56 ml) water
7 oz (198 g) creamed coconut
4 eggs
¼ teaspoonful grated nutmeg
½ teaspoonful grated lemon rind (optional)

Place the jaggery in a pan with the water and boil until it has dissolved. Strain and pour the liquid jaggery back into the pan. Dissolve the creamed coconut in the jaggery and allow to cool. Whisk the eggs and pour into the milk mixture. Pour the mixture into a bowl, add nutmeg and lemon rind and cover. Steam for 2 hours.

Serves 4–6

Payasam

A nourishing and tasty Indian milk dessert.

1 oz (28 g) roasted vermicelli (available at Indian grocery stores)
1 oz (28 g) butter
26 fl oz (738 ml) milk
2½ tablespoonsful sugar
1 oz (28 g) chopped blanched almonds
4 drops almond essence
¼ teaspoonful saffron powder
6 cardamoms

Break the vermicelli into 2 in (5 cm) strands. Heat the butter and gently fry the vermicelli until pale brown. Add the milk and sugar and bring to the boil. Lower the heat and simmer for 20 minutes, stirring at regular intervals. When the mixture resembles thick porridge, add the nuts, almond essence, saffron and the crushed cardamom seeds. Cook for a further 3 minutes. The sweet is best served at room temperature, due to the fat content.

Serves 4

Gulab Jamun

An Indian dessert made of flour and milk solids, served with a light sugar syrup.

1 oz (28 g) butter
2 oz (56 g) self-raising flour
4 oz (113 g) full cream milk powder
1 fl oz (28 ml) milk
oil or ghee for deep frying

Syrup
8 oz (226 g) sugar
2 cups water
1 tablespoonful rose water

In a bowl mix the butter and flour to resemble fine breadcrumbs.
Add the milk powder. Gradually work in the milk to form a stiff
dough. Knead the dough thoroughly. Divide into twenty portions
and form into balls. Heat the oil or ghee and over a *very* low heat
fry the gulab jamuns about four at a time. They will increase in
size and gradually turn a dark brown colour. Drain on kitchen
paper. (If the gulab jamuns split during frying either the oil is too
hot or the dough has not been kneaded sufficiently.)

Place the sugar and water in a large pan and bring rapidly to the
boil. Reduce the heat and simmer for 5 minutes. Remove from the
heat and allow to cool slightly. Add the rose water and lastly the
gulab jamuns. Allow the gulab jamuns to soak in the syrup for a
couple of hours before serving cold.

Serves 6

Rasagullas

Yet another sweetmeat made of milk. A popular Indian dessert.

2 pints (1.2 l) milk
juice of a lemon
2 teaspoonsful semolina
2 cups sugar
4 cups water
2 tablespoonsful rose water

Bring the milk to the boil. Add the lemon juice to it. The milk will
curdle and the cheese will separate from the whey. Pour through a
muslin or soft cloth and allow to drain. Squeeze out as much of the
liquid as possible. The milk solids or cheese that is left in the cloth
is then thoroughly kneaded together with the semolina. Divide into
twelve portions and form into small balls. Boil the sugar and water

in a pan. Once the sugar has dissolved and the syrup has been boiled for 5 minutes, divide the syrup into two. Allow half the quantity to cool and boil the rest. Once it is boiling add the cheese balls to the boiling sugar syrup and allow to continue boiling for 20 minutes. Remove the cheese balls and put into the cold syrup. Add the rose water. Reheat on a low heat for 10 minutes before serving.

Serves 6

Burfi

A traditional Indian sweetmeat made of concentrated milk cheese, butter and nuts.

2 pints (1.2 l) milk
juice of a lemon
icing sugar
2 oz (56 g) butter
2 oz (56 g) milk powder
2 oz (56 g) ground almonds
6 drops almond essence
castor sugar

Boil the milk. Add the lemon juice and boil for a further 3 minutes. Strain in a muslin and allow the whey to drip away. On a board dusted with icing sugar, lightly knead the curds, butter, milk powder, the ground almonds and essence until the mixture is smooth. Weigh this mixture and add three-quarters its weight in castor sugar. Place in a pan and cook over a low heat for 20 minutes. Place on a buttered dish and cut into 1 in (2.5 cm) squares.

Serves 8

Jalebis

A lighter version of the Indian sweetmeat burfi, served in a heavy sugar syrup

$1\frac{1}{2}$ teacups plain flour
3 tablespoonsful plain yoghurt
$\frac{3}{4}$ cup water

½ teaspoonful saffron powder
2 cups sugar
2 cups water
1 pint (568 ml) oil

Mix the flour and the yoghurt. Gradually add the three-quarter cup
of water and beat to a smooth batter. Add the saffron. Leave the
batter covered in a warm place for about 10 hours. Boil the sugar
and water over a low heat and keep warm until the jalebis are
fried. Heat the fat to smoking. Fill a funnel with the batter and
pour spirals of the batter into the hot fat. When brown on both
sides put into the sugar syrup. When they are soaked in the syrup
place in a dish. Jalebis can be eaten hot or cold.

Serves 8

Masur Pak

This is an oily, rich Indian sweet.

3 oz (85 g) clarified butter or ghee
4 oz (113 g) sugar
4 fl oz (113 ml) water
1½ tablespoonsful gram flour
1½ tablespoonsful ground almonds
6 cardamom pods
sliced almonds for decoration

Place the fat, sugar and water in a pan. Bring to the boil and allow
to cook for 5 minutes. Reduce the heat and into this sizzling
mixture gradually beat in the sieved flour. Care should be taken to
thoroughly mix each addition of flour. Add the ground almonds
and lastly the crushed cardamom seeds. Stir for about 7 minutes on
a low heat until the mixture leaves the sides of the pan. Spread on
a dish and decorate with almonds.

Makes 16 pieces, serves 8

Semolina Halva

A delicious Indian dessert made of semolina and milk.

11 oz (310 g) coarse semolina
4 oz (113 g) butter or ghee
1 pint (568 ml) milk

7 tablespoonsful sugar
2 oz (56 g) blanched almonds
a few drops of almond essence
¼ teaspoonful saffron powder

Over a low heat, stirring continuously, roast the semolina until pale brown. Add the butter, milk and sugar and stir continuously to prevent the semolina sticking to the pan. When quite stiff add the almonds, the essence and the saffron which has been dissolved in ¼ teaspoonful of water. Mix thoroughly and pat onto a buttered tray to about ¼ in (6 mm) thick. Cut into 1 in (2.5 cm) squares.

Serves 8

Srikhand

A light and refreshing dessert to finish an Indian meal.

4 cups natural unsweetened yoghurt
3 oz (85 g) castor sugar
½ teaspoonful saffron powder
¼ teaspoonful ground cardamom
1 oz (28 g) flaked almonds for garnishing

Pour the yoghurt into a fine muslin cloth and allow the whey to drain away by hanging the muslin over the sink for about 6 hours. Scrape the yoghurt solids into a bowl. Beat in the sugar either by hand with a wooden spoon or with an electric blender until the yoghurt mixture is smooth. Dissolve the saffron in a teaspoonful of hot water. Add the dissolved saffron and the ground cardamoms. Garnish with the flaked almonds and serve well chilled.

Serves 4

Love Cake

An exotic Sri Lankan recipe, reputed to have been handed down from the Dutch! This is an unusual spicy cake with a nutty flavour and can be stored in an airtight container for about a month.

8 oz (226 g) butter
8 oz (226 g) semolina
10 egg yolks
1 lb (454 g) soft brown sugar
1 teaspoonful grated nutmeg
1 teaspoonful grated lemon rind
½ teaspoonful powdered cinnamon
1 tablespoonful rose water
2 teaspoonsful vanilla essence
1 tablespoonful honey
12 oz (340 g) cashewnuts, minced or finely chopped
2 egg whites, whisked

Soften the butter and gradually mix in the semolina. Leave in a warm place so that the semolina is soaked into the butter. Cream the egg yolks and gradually beat in the sugar until light and creamy. Add the spices, rose water, vanilla and honey. Beat in the semolina and butter. Add the nuts and lastly fold in the whites of the eggs. Pour into a lined rectangular cake tin, 12 × 12 in (30 × 30 cm) and bake at Gas Mark 5/375°F for 2½ hours. Cut into squares before serving.

Almond Biscuits

A Chinese sweetmeat.

4 oz (113 g) lard
4 oz (113 g) castor sugar
1 egg
1 teaspoonful almond essence
6 oz (168 g) plain flour
½ teaspoonful baking powder
a pinch of salt
blanched split almond halves for decoration
a beaten egg for glazing

Cream the lard and sugar until light. Add the egg and beat thoroughly. Add the almond essence. Sift the flour, baking powder and salt, and use your fingers to mix them into the beaten mixture to form a stiff dough. Chill the dough for half an hour. Using the palms of your hands form little balls of dough. Flatten the dough balls to form a circular shape and place on a greased baking sheet. Press half an almond on to each biscuit, brush with beaten egg and bake at Gas Mark 4/350°F for 12–15 minutes.

Makes 35–40 biscuits

Toffee Apples

These are popular with children and are eaten in Singapore and China alike.

4 oz (113 g) plain flour
1 egg, lightly beaten
5 fl oz (142 ml) cold water
2 firm eating apples
8 oz (226 g) granulated sugar
1 tablespoonful oil
2 teaspoonsful sesame seeds
oil for deep frying
a bowl of iced water with some ice cubes

Sieve the flour into a bowl. Mix the egg and the cold water and gradually work it into the flour until you have a smooth batter. Peel the apples and cut each apple into quarters. Remove the core and cut each quarter into two. In a heavy bottomed medium sized saucepan bring the sugar, the tablespoonful of oil and 4 fl oz (113 ml) of water to the boil. Continue to boil rapidly until the syrup has thickened and caramelized. Add the sesame seeds. Leave on a low heat. Heat the oil for deep frying until it is smoking hot. Lightly grease a serving plate. Coat about six apple pieces in the batter and drop into the hot oil. Allow to fry until pale brown. Lift out with a slotted spoon and put into the sugar syrup. When coated with the syrup put immediately into the bowl of iced water to harden. Remove immediately and place on the greased plate. Repeat the process until all the apple pieces are used up. Serve at once.

Serves 4

11

Savoury Snacks
&
Side Dishes

Pappadam

A versatile side dish or snack, or a crisp accompaniment for any curry meal, pappadams are prepared from ready made packets easily available from Indian food stores. They can be stored in an airtight tin for a few days. There are several varieties of pappadams on the market; the spiced ones are particularly delicious.

1 packet pappadam
oil for deep frying

Using a pair of scissors cut each pappadam into four equal pieces. Heat the oil until it is smoking hot. Put in a pappadam. In a couple of seconds the pappadam will expand and rise to the surface. Turn over and allow to fry for two seconds. Drain on kitchen paper. The frying should be done very quickly to prevent the pappadams from burning. Allow about four pieces per person.

Krupuk (Indonesian Prawn Crisps)

These prawn crackers are made of tapioca flour which is mixed with fish, shrimps and spices, steamed, sliced and dried before being packeted. An important accompaniment to any Indonesian meal, they are available in Chinese shops and need to be fried in deep hot fat before serving. They are delicious as an accompaniment to drinks.

Rempeyek Katjang (Peanut Fritters)

An Indonesian speciality, these peanut fritters are eaten with a rice and curry meal. They are also delicious on their own as a snack. If raw peanuts are unobtainable use unsalted peanuts.

6 oz (168 g) ground rice
1 teaspoonful salt
1 small onion, finely chopped
1 clove garlic, crushed
2 teaspoonsful coriander powder
½ teaspoonful cumin powder
½ teaspoonful turmeric

3 oz (85 g) creamed coconut
8 oz (226 g) raw or unsalted peanuts
oil for deep frying

In a bowl mix the rice, salt, onion, garlic and spices. Dissolve the creamed coconut in a cup of boiling water. Allow to cool. If using raw peanuts pour boiling water over them and remove the skins. Mix the coconut milk into the dry ingredients to form a smooth batter. Add the peanuts. Heat the oil and drop spoonsful of the batter into the hot oil and fry until golden brown on both sides. Drain on paper and when cold store in an airtight container.

Serves 6–8

Rempeyek Udang

Indonesian prawn fritters.

6 oz (168 g) rice flour
1 teaspoonful salt
2 teaspoonsful coriander powder
$\frac{1}{2}$ teaspoonful cumin powder
$\frac{1}{4}$ teaspoonful chilli powder
2 cloves garlic, chopped
1 small onion, finely chopped
2 oz (56 g) creamed coconut
6 oz (168 g) prawns or shrimps
1 egg, beaten
oil for deep frying

In a bowl mix the rice flour, salt, spices, garlic and onion. Dissolve the creamed coconut in half a cup of boiling water. Allow to get cold. Shell and de-vein the prawns and chop into small pieces. Mix the beaten egg with the coconut milk and gradually add it to the dry ingredients to form a fairly stiff batter. Add the prawns or shrimps. Heat the oil until it is hot. Drop spoonsful of the batter and fry until brown on both sides. Drain on paper and serve.

Serves 6–8

Wontons

A recipe for wonton wrappers is given on p. 16. Wonton wrappers are also available in Chinese supermarkets and are filled with a seasoned minced pork and seafood mixture. They can be deep fried

or steamed and eaten as a snack or boiled in stock to make
'wonton soup' (see p. 32).

12 oz (340 g) lean pork, very finely minced
2 oz (56 g) fresh prawns, very finely chopped
1 teaspoonful salt
1 tablespoonful soy sauce
3 spring onions, very finely sliced
1 teaspoonful fresh ginger, grated
8 oz (226 g) wonton wrappers

In a bowl mix together the pork, prawns, salt, soy sauce, spring
onions and ginger. Take a wonton wrapper and place about three-
quarters of a teaspoonful of the filling in the centre. Fold over the
wrapper and seal the edges so that you have a shape that nearly
resembles a triangle. Now take the two base points of the triangle
and pinch together with moistened fingers. If it is difficult to make
this complicated shape, just stick to a simple triangular one. While
you are making them keep the wrappers and the prepared
dumplings covered in a damp cloth. They can be deep fried,
steamed or boiled.

Makes about 30–35

Pakoda (Savoury Vegetable Fritters)

An Indian teatime snack which could also be served as an
accompaniment to a meal. The batter should be mixed just prior to
use.

5 oz (140 g) gram flour
1 teaspoonful salt
½ teaspoonful chilli powder
¼ teaspoonful turmeric
¼ teaspoonful baking powder
6 fl oz (170 ml) water
1 potato
2 onions
2 green peppers
oil for deep frying

Sieve the gram flour into a bowl. Add the next four ingredients,
then gradually add the water to form a thick batter. Beat until
smooth. Cut the vegetables into bite-sized pieces. Dip the vegetable

pieces into the batter – a few at a time – and deep fry in smoking hot oil until golden brown.

Alternatively finely shred three medium onions and mix into the batter. Drop spoonfuls of the mixture into the hot oil and fry until golden brown. Serve hot with chutney or ketchup.

Serves 6–8

Spring Rolls

A good start to a Chinese or Far Eastern meal, or a savoury snack with drinks.

wonton wrappers (see BASIC RECIPES*)*
8 oz (226 g) pork tenderloin
8 oz (226 g) shelled prawns or shrimps
8 oz (226 g) bean sprouts
5 spring onions
1 dessertspoonful cornflour
1 tablespoonful soy sauce
1 teaspoonful salt
½ teaspoonful sugar
1 tablespoonful Chinese rice wine or dry sherry
oil for deep frying

Roll out the pastry and cut into 6 in (15 cm) squares. Store the pastry squares between sheets of greaseproof paper in a plastic container in the refrigerator.

Chop the pork into very fine pieces. Chop the prawns or shrimps into small pieces. Wash and drain the bean sprouts. Finely slice the spring onions. Mix the cornflour with a dessertspoonful of cold water. Heat a wok or frying pan over a medium heat. Add a tablespoonful of oil to it. When the oil is smoking hot add the pork pieces and stir fry for a minute. Then add the prawns or shrimps and stir continuously for a further minute. Lastly add the bean sprouts and the spring onions and continue to cook for about 2 minutes. Add the soy sauce, salt, sugar and wine and mix thoroughly. Lastly add the cornflour mixture and stir until the liquid has thickened. Allow the mixture to cool to room temperature before making the rolls.

Take a pastry square and place two teaspoonsful of the filling roughly in a cylindrical shape diagonally across the centre of the square. Tuck one of the corners at right angles to the filling over and under the filling. Fold the corners on either side of the filling over tightly so that the parcel resembles an open envelope. Roll the bulk of the parcel to the edge until you have a neat cylindrical shape. Moisten the edge with cold water and seal. Repeat until all the filling has been used up. Heat the oil for deep frying until it is smoking hot. Deep fry three or four spring rolls at a time until golden brown and crisp. Drain on kitchen paper. Serve hot.

Makes 12–16

Rum

Savoury stuffed omelette, Thai style.

1 oz (28 g) lard or vegetable oil
3 cloves garlic, finely chopped
8 oz (226 g) lean pork, minced
1 tablespoonful fish sauce (nam pla)
½ teaspoonful sugar
¼ teaspoonful salt
¼ teaspoonful freshly milled black pepper
2 eggs, well beaten
1 tablespoonful coriander leaves
2 red chillies, de-seeded and finely sliced

Heat the lard or oil and brown the garlic in it. Add the pork and stir fry until cooked. Add the fish sauce, sugar, salt and pepper. Cook for about 3 minutes and allow to get cold. Lightly grease an omelette pan and pour just enough beaten egg to coat the surface of the pan. Allow to cook and turn over and cook on the other side. Put the omelette on a plate and arrange a few coriander leaves on it. Add a tablespoonful of the meat mixture, a few pieces of sliced chilli and neatly fold the omelette over to form a parcel. Repeat the cooking process until all the egg has been used.

Serves 4

Dashi-maki Tamago (Rolled Omelette)

In Japan a rectangular pan is used to make this rolled omelette which rather resembles a swiss roll. It can be successfully made in a frying pan which is about 1 in (2.5 cm) deep. Care should be taken to cook the egg mixture on a medium to low heat so that the outside layer remains yellow and not brown.

4 eggs
3 fl oz (85 ml) dashi
2 teaspoonsful soy sauce
½ teaspoonful salt
½ teaspoonful sugar
groundnut oil
parsley for garnishing

Break the eggs into a bowl and beat well. Add the dashi, soy sauce, salt and sugar, and beat until thoroughly mixed. Heat a pan about 9 in (23 cm) in diameter. Grease the pan well with oil and pour a third of the egg mixture into the pan. Tilt in a circular motion so the egg mixture evenly covers the surface of the pan. When the egg mixture has barely set, roll the omelette away from you into a neat cylindrical shape. Leave this omelette roll in the pan. Grease the pan again and move the rolled omelette nearest to you. Pour half the egg mixture and swirl it in the pan so it covers the entire surface of the pan. Once the mixture begins to set roll the omelette, so as to wrap the newly cooked layer of omelette making a thicker cylindrical egg roll. Repeat this process with the remaining egg mixture. You should now have a wide cylindrical omelette roll. Place this while hot on a clean tea towel and wrap it securely in order to hold the cylindrical shape. Allow to cool and cut into thick even slices as you would a swiss roll. Garnish with parsley.

Serves 4

Dadar Jawa (Omelette the Javanese way)

4 eggs
½ teaspoonful salt
1 teaspoonful soy sauce
½ teaspoonful brown sugar
oil for frying
1 small onion, finely chopped
2 fresh chillies, finely chopped

Beat the eggs. Add the salt, soy sauce and brown sugar. Heat a heavy bottomed large frying pan. Add a tablespoonful of oil. When the oil is hot fry the onions in it. Add the chillies and the egg mixture. Allow the omelette to brown on the bottom. Carefully tip out onto a plate and serve warm.

Serves 2–3

Pazoon Ngabaung Jaw

This delicious Burmese prawn snack is easy to prepare and could be served as a starter or an accompaniment to a main course.

1 cup chick pea flour
1 teaspoonful salt
¼ teaspoonful bicarbonate of soda
¼ teaspoonful turmeric
¼ teaspoonful chilli powder (optional)
4–6 fl oz (113–170 ml) tepid water
1 clove garlic, finely chopped
1 teaspoonful ginger, finely chopped
14 oz (410 g) tinned or frozen shrimps
oil for deep frying

Sieve the flour into a mixing bowl. Add the salt, bicarbonate of soda, turmeric and chilli powder. Gradually add the water and beat until smooth. Add the garlic, ginger and prawns. Heat the oil over a medium heat. Drop spoonsful of the mixture into hot oil and fry until golden brown. Drain on kitchen paper and serve warm.

Serves 4–6

Sankhaya (Steamed Custard)

This Thai custard is steamed in a pumpkin or a young coconut, but when neither is available it can be steamed in a bowl or individual cups.

4 oz (113 g) creamed coconut
1 cup water
3 eggs
5 oz (142 g) palm sugar or soft dark brown sugar
a pinch of salt
1 pumpkin, about 9 in (23 cm) in diameter

Put the creamed coconut and water in a pan. Over a low heat dissolve the creamed coconut, stirring constantly to prevent it from burning. Beat the eggs and add the sugar to them. Add the cooled creamed coconut and salt. Wash the pumpkin and cut about 2 in (5 cm) off the top. Using a metal spoon remove the seeds and the tissue. Strain and pour the custard into the pumpkin.

Place the pumpkin in a bowl so that it stands upright quite securely. Place the bowl in a colander and steam for about $1\frac{1}{2}$ hours or until the custard has set. Cool and chill thoroughly. Cut into slices and serve.

Serves 4–6

Be-ya-jaw (Split Pea Rissoles)

A Burmese speciality, these lentil rissoles can also be served with drinks. Larger versions are sometimes crumbled over a hot noodle soup.

1 cup split peas
1½ teaspoonsful salt
1 medium onion, finely chopped
½ teaspoonful chilli powder
oil for deep frying

Wash the split peas thoroughly and soak overnight in cold water. Drain away the water and grind in a blender until the mixture resembles a coarse paste. Mix in the salt, onions and chilli powder. Heat the oil over a medium heat. Mould a dessertspoonful of the lentil paste to resemble a mini hamburger and deep fry until browned. Drain on kitchen paper.

Makes 24, serves 6

Masala Vade (Lentil Rissoles)

This South Indian snack is also popular among the Tamils of Sri Lanka. It provides a nourishing teatime savoury.

1 cup masur dhal (orange lentils)
1½ teaspoonsful powdered dry fish (optional)
¼ teaspoonful turmeric powder

½ teaspoonful chilli powder
1 teaspoonful salt
1 medium onion, finely chopped
10 curry leaves (or bay leaves), broken in small pieces
vegetable oil for deep frying
3 green chillies, finely chopped

Wash the dhal in cold water several times, place in a bowl with
one cup of cold water and allow to soak for 3 hours. Grind the dhal
in a blender. Mix in all the other ingredients. Drop dessertspoonsful
of the thick lentil batter into the hot fat. Turn and brown on both
sides. Drain on kitchen paper and serve hot. Yields about 25.

Serves 5

Patties (Savoury Pastries)

A Sri Lankan party snack, served with drinks. Could also be served
as a starter.

1 lb (454 g) plain flour
1 teaspoonful baking powder
1½ teaspoonsful salt
2 oz (56 g) margarine
1 egg, beaten
6–8 fl oz (170–225 ml) cold water
oil for deep frying

Sieve the flour and the baking powder into a bowl. Add the salt.
Rub in the margarine to resemble fine breadcrumbs. Make a well in
the centre of the flour and work in the beaten egg and sufficient
water to form a stiff dough. Mix thoroughly and leave in a cool
place for half an hour.

Filling
1 tablespoonful oil
1 onion, finely chopped
⅛ teaspoonful turmeric
1 teaspoonful coriander powder
1 teaspoonful cumin powder
12 oz (340 g) lean minced meat
1 teaspoonful fresh ginger, chopped
4 cloves garlic, chopped
1 potato, diced very finely
1 tomato, chopped
¾ teaspoonful salt
1 oz (28 g) creamed coconut dissolved in 2 fl oz (56 ml) hot water

Heat the oil and fry the onion until golden brown. Add the spices, the meat, the ginger and garlic and fry on a low heat for about 5 minutes. Add the potato, tomato, salt and lastly the creamed coconut. Bring to the boil and cover and simmer for 20 minutes on a very low heat. Since a dry curry is required, care should be taken to ensure that the meat does not stick to the pan by stirring the meat at regular intervals. Remove from the heat and cool thoroughly.

On a dusted board or table roll out half the pastry to the thickness of a fine pancake. Using a pastry cutter about 4 in (10 cm) in diameter cut out rounds of pastry. Place a small quantity of the filling in the centre. Moisten the edges with cold water and seal. Using a table fork press round the sealed edge to make sure that the patty is well sealed or else it will open during frying. Repeat the rolling until all the pastry is used. Heat the oil until it is smoking hot. Put in about five patties at a time and fry until golden brown. Drain on kitchen paper and serve hot.

Makes about 50

Samosas (Indian Vegetable Pasties)

An excellent short-eat or snack to be served with drinks, or as a starter to a main course.

8 oz (226 g) plain flour
½ teaspoonful salt
2 tablespoonsful melted ghee or oil
approximately 1 cup yoghurt
oil for deep frying

Sieve the flour into a bowl with the salt. Make a well in the centre of the flour and work in the ghee and sufficient yoghurt to form a stiff smooth dough. Leave covered in a cool place while the filling is made.

Filling
1 tablespoonful oil or ghee
1 onion, finely chopped
¼ teaspoonful garam masala
¼ teaspoonful coriander powder
¼ teaspoonful cumin powder
½ teaspoonful ginger, finely chopped

1 cup mashed potato
½ cup cooked peas
½ teaspoonful salt

Heat the oil and fry the onions until lightly browned. Add the spices and the rest of the ingredients and mix thoroughly. Allow the filling to cool.

On a dusted board roll out the pastry. Using a pastry cutter or glass of 4 in (10 cm) diameter, cut out circles of pastry. Place a small quantity of the filling in the centre. Moisten the edges with cold water and seal. Using a table fork press round the sealed edge to ensure that the pasty is well sealed. Repeat the rolling until all the pastry is used. Heat the oil until it is smoking hot. Fry a few pasties at a time. Drain on kitchen paper and serve hot with chutney or ketchup.

Makes 30

12

Relishes & Sambols

Thanhut (Burmese Cucumber Relish)

3 large green cucumbers
4 tablespoonsful vinegar
2 tablespoonsful sesame seeds
10 cloves garlic
1 medium onion
½ cup sesame oil
1 teaspoonful turmeric
1½ teaspoonsful salt
½ teaspoonful sugar

Peel the cucumbers and cut them lengthwise into two. Remove the seeds and cut into 2½ in long (6.4 cm) julienne strips about ¾ in (2 cm) in width. In a pan bring three cups of water and the vinegar to the boil. Blanch the cucumbers in this for a couple of minutes or until they are transparent. Drain away the water and allow to cool. In a small heavy bottomed pan, over a medium heat, dry roast the sesame seeds until golden brown. Remove from the pan and allow to cool.

Peel and finely slice the garlic and the onion. Deep fry the garlic and the onion in the sesame oil until golden brown. Allow to cool. In a non-metallic bowl toss the cucumbers in the turmeric, salt, sugar and three tablespoonsful of the cooled oil. Garnish with the garlic, onion and sesame seeds.

Serves 6

Atjar Ketimun (Pickled Cucumber)

An Indonesian relish.

4 green cucumbers
1–1½ teaspoonsful salt
4 red chillies
3 tablespoonsful sugar
1 pint (568 ml) white vinegar

Wash the cucumbers and cut each lengthwise into four. Remove the seeds and cut into small cubes. Sprinkle with salt and leave for half an hour. Drain away the water and add the sliced chillies to it. In a pan heat the sugar and vinegar together and stir over a low heat until the sugar has dissolved. Allow to cool. Mix the cucumbers in the vinegar and serve.

Serves 8–10

Sambal Kelapa (Indonesian Sambol)

4 oz (56 g) fresh or desiccated coconut
4 red chillies
1 small onion
1 clove garlic
½ teaspoonful dried shrimp paste (trasi)
½ teaspoonful salt
1 teaspoonful lime or lemon juice

If using fresh coconut, grate the coconut finely. If using desiccated coconut, moisten by mixing in two tablespoonsful of hot water. Using a pestle and mortar or an electric blender grind the chillies, onion and garlic to a smooth paste. Crush the trasi. Mix all the ingredients together and stir well.

Khayan-chindi-Jaw (Tomato Relish)

A rather strongly flavoured Burmese relish.

1½ lb (680 g) tomatoes
2 medium onions
4 cloves garlic
2 tablespoonsful light sesame oil or any vegetable oil
1 teaspoonful turmeric
4 teaspoonsful dried prawns, powdered or ground

Wash and cut the tomatoes into quarters. Finely slice the onions and garlic. Heat the oil in a saucepan over medium heat. Add the onions and garlic and fry until lightly browned. Add the tomatoes, turmeric and prawns. Bring to the boil and simmer, covered, for about 10 minutes. Serve cold.

Serves 6–8

Seeni Sambol

This is a Sri Lankan speciality and is relished as an accompaniment to any rice and curry meal. It is eaten in small quantities, and loosely translated means sugar sambol despite the many other ingredients that go to make it.

oil for deep frying
1½ lb (680 g) onions, finely sliced
½ oz (14 g) tamarind
1 tablespoonful oil
1½ tablespoonsful maldive fish or dried prawns (optional)
4 cloves garlic, finely chopped
1½ teaspoonsful ginger, finely chopped
1 oz (28 g) creamed coconut, dissolved in ½ cup of boiling water
1½ teaspoonsful salt
1 tablespoonful chilli powder
1 teaspoonful sugar
4 cardamom pods
2 pieces cinnamon stick

Heat the oil and deep fry the onions, a few at a time until golden brown. Drain on absorbent paper. Soak the tamarind in half a cup of water for about 20 minutes. Put the tamarind and the water into a pan and cook on a low heat for about 5 minutes. Strain the tamarind liquid and set aside. In a small pan heat the tablespoonful of oil and add the maldive fish or prawns to it. Allow to fry for about 5 minutes. Add the garlic, ginger and the rest of the ingredients, including the tamarind water. Bring to the boil and simmer on a very low heat until the liquid has evaporated.

Serundeng

This Indonesian peanut and coconut garnish is served as an accompaniment to a rice meal and can be stored in an airtight container for a week.

1 cup desiccated coconut
1 teaspoonful ground cumin
½ teaspoonful dried shrimp paste
1 teaspoonful ground coriander
1 small onion, very finely chopped
1 dessertspoonful tamarind water or lemon juice
2 cloves garlic, very finely chopped

1 teaspoonful fresh ginger, finely chopped
3 tablespoonsful peanut oil
½ teaspoonful salt
4 oz (56 g) roasted peanuts

In a bowl mix the coconut, cumin, shrimp paste, coriander, onion,
tamarind water, garlic and ginger. Coat the surface of a heavy
bottomed frying pan with the oil and fry the coconut mixture over
a low heat until golden brown. During the frying the mixture
should be stirred constantly to prevent it burning. Add the salt. Mix
in the peanuts. Serve cold.

Serves 6–8

Dried Prawn Sambol

A Sri Lankan speciality, an ideal accompaniment to rice dishes,
particularly pilafs.

2 oz (56 g) dried prawns
1 cup oil
8 oz (226 g) onions, finely sliced
3 cloves garlic, chopped
½ teaspoonful fresh ginger, chopped
½ teaspoonful salt
½ teaspoonful chilli powder
1 dessertspoonful lemon juice

Wash the prawns, place in an ovenproof dish and roast at Gas
Mark ½/200°F for 1 hour. Grind the prawns in an electric blender.
Heat the oil and fry the finely sliced onion until golden brown.
Drain the onions on kitchen paper. In another pan heat one
tablespoonful of oil and fry the garlic and ginger for 3 minutes. Add
the dried prawn powder and continue to fry on a low heat for
about 5 minutes. Add the salt and the chilli powder and lastly the
onions, and mix thoroughly. Remove from the heat and add the
lemon juice.

Serves 6

Kapi Pla (Shrimp Relish)

A Thai relish that is an excellent accompaniment to a spicy main
course.

4 tablespoonsful dried shrimp paste
1 small onion, finely chopped
5 cloves garlic, finely chopped
1 oz (28 g) dried prawns, ground
2 fl oz (56 ml) lemon or lime juice
1 dessertspoonful sugar
1½ tablespoonsful fish sauce
2 fresh red chillies, finely sliced for garnishing
1 teaspoonful grated lemon or lime rind, for garnishing

Wrap the shrimp paste in tin foil and bake in a hot oven (Gas Mark 4/350°F) for 5 minutes. Allow to cool. Using either a pestle and mortar or an electric blender, blend together the first seven ingredients. Pile into a bowl and garnish with the red chillies and grated rind.

Nga-pi-Jaw (Fried Chillies)

This is a very hot Burmese sambol and should be eaten in very small quantities.

4 oz (113 g) dried red chillies
2 tablespoonsful oil
2 teaspoonsful dried prawn powder
¼ teaspoonful salt

In a heavy bottomed frying pan, over a low heat, dry roast the chillies. Coarsely grind the chillies in an electric blender. Heat the oil in a frying pan. Add the prawn powder and stir fry over a medium heat for a minute. Add the chillies and continue to stir for a further minute. Add the salt. Cool on a plate and serve with curries.

Sambal Ulek (Hot Chillies Ground)

A hot Indonesian sambol, served as an accompaniment to a rice meal. Be warned: eat it in very small quantities!

2 tablespoonsful oil
12 large red chillies
1 small onion, chopped
1 clove garlic, chopped

1 teaspoonful brown sugar
½ teaspoonful salt

Heat the oil and fry the chillies, onion and garlic in it. Allow to get cold. Grind all the ingredients in an electric blender.

Sambal Bajak

An Indonesian sambol. Serve as an accompaniment to any rice meal. It can be stored in an airtight container in the refrigerator.

10 large red chillies
1 large onion
2 cloves garlic
1 teaspoonful dried shrimp paste (trasi)
2 tablespoonsful peanut oil
2 teaspoonsful brown sugar
2 kemiri nuts, when available
1 teaspoonful salt

Grind the chillies, onion and garlic to a smooth paste. Using the back of a spoon crush the shrimp paste. Heat the oil in a pan and fry the ground ingredients until cooked. Add the rest of the ingredients and continue cooking until the oil separates from the mixture. Allow to get cold.

Menu Suggestions

I list below a selection of main course combinations grouped under different countries. Together with the large number of soups, starters and sweets I have included in my recipes very many exotic menus can be devised. Of course, there is no good reason to stick to recipes from any one country in planning a menu. Hybrid menu combinations are to be strongly recommended and would, I think, provide an exciting range of possibilities.

Burma

Burmese Mixed Noodles
Burmese Chicken Curry
Khayan – chindi – Jaw (Tomato Relish)
Pazoon Ngabaung Jaw (Prawn Snack)

Panthay Kaukswe (Chicken Curry)
Cellophane Noodles
Thanhut (Burmese Cucumber Relish)

Ame Hnat (Braised Beef)
Boiled Rice
Nga-pi-Jaw (Fried Chillies)

China

Chicken with Chestnuts
Boiled Rice
Stir Fried Cabbage
Cha-yeh-tan (Tea-leaf Eggs)

Cha-chiang-mein (Boiled Egg Noodles with Meat Sauce)
Pork Spareribs
Liang-pan-huang-kua (Cucumber Salad in a Spicy Dressing)

Chinese Barbecued Chicken
Boiled Rice
Stir Fried Snow Peas with Mushrooms

Yin-ya-chi-ssu (Stir Fried Chicken with Fresh Bean Sprouts)
Boiled Rice
Hsia-mi-pan Ch'in-ts'ai (Celery and Dried Shrimp Salad)

Sweet and Sour Pork
Boiled Rice
Stir Fried Cabbage
Spring Rolls

Peking Duck
Boiled Rice
Liang-pan-huang-kua (Cucumber Salad in a Spicy Dressing)

India

Vegetable Biriani
Cauliflower, Stuffed
Moong Dhal with Spinach
Pappadams

Chicken Biriani
Curried Aubergines
Onion Salad

Kashmiri Lamb with Dried Fruit
Boiled Rice
Spinach, Stir Fried
Leeks in Gram Flour

Tandouri Chicken
Chappatis
Lettuce with Peanut Dressing
Thur Dhal
Pickles

Mulligatawny
Kebabs
Boiled Rice
Stuffed Bhindi

Kichiri
Spicy Fried Chicken
Onion Salad

Chicken, Kashmiri-style
Puris and Boiled Rice
Cauliflower, Stuffed

Fish in Yoghurt Sauce
Boiled Rice
Leeks in Gram Flour

Indonesia

Sate Ayam (Chicken Sate)
Boiled Rice
Sayur Tumis (Stir Fried Vegetables)

Sate Babi (Pork Sate)
Nasi Kuning (Yellow Rice)
Sayur Tumis (Stir Fried Vegetables)

Bamie Goreng (Mixed Fried Noodles)
Ayam Kuning (Dry Chicken Curry)
Selada Tomat

Nasi Gurih (Coconut Milk Rice)
Ayam Pang gang (Grilled Chicken)
Sayur Lodeh (Mixed Vegetable Curry)

Sate Pandang
Boiled Rice
Selada Udang (Prawn Salad)

Selada Husar (Beef with Pineapple Salad)
Nasi Goreng
Tahu Goreng (Spicy Bean Curd Salad)

Gule Ikan (Fish Curry)
Boiled Rice
Sayur Asam (Sour Mixed Vegetables)

Ikan Bali (Balinese Fish)
Boiled Rice
Gado-Gado (Mixed Vegetables with Peanut Sauce)

Japan

Chicken Teriyaki
Zaru Soba
Boiled Rice

Toriniku Tatsuate-Age (Marinaded Deep Fried Chicken)
Oden
Boiled Rice

Mizutaki
Boiled Rice

Sukiyaki
Boiled Rice

Yakitori (Kebabs)
Boiled Rice

Sri Lanka

Kaha Bath
Uru Mas Curry (Pork)
Curried Aubergines
Dried Prawn Sambol

Kiri Bath
Seeni Sambol
Harak Mas Curry (Beef)
Cashewnut Curry

String Hopper Pilau
Kukul Mas Curry (Chicken)
Pickles

Dosa (Lentil Pancakes)
Curried Aubergines
Parippu (Lentil Curry)

Prawn Curry
Boiled Rice
Cashewnut Curry

Thailand

Kai Panen (Chicken in Coconut)
Phat Wun Sen (Mixed Fried Rice Sticks)
Thai Vegetable Salad

Kaeng Massaman (Muslim Curry)
Mi Krob (Crisp Fried Rice Sticks)
Thai Cucumber Salad

Ma Ho (Galloping Horses)
Stir Fried Snow Peas with Pork
Fried Beehoon

Thai Fried Shrimp and Broccoli
Mie Siam
Thai Cucumber Salad

Ho Mok (Steamed Fish)
Khao Phat (Fried Rice)
Kapi Pla (Shrimp Relish)

Red Curry of Shrimp
Kai Kwam (Stuffed Fried Eggs)
Boiled Rice

Index